Love in the Hebrew Bible

Love in the Hebrew Bible

Song-Mi Suzie Park

WESTMINSTER
JOHN KNOX PRESS
LOUISVILLE • KENTUCKY

First edition
Published by Westminster John Knox Press
Louisville, Kentucky

23 24 25 26 27 28 29 30 31 32—10 9 8 7 6 5 4 3 2 1

Book design by Sharon Adams
Cover design by Allison Taylor
Cover Art: David and King Saul *by Leslie Xuereb / UIG / Bridgeman Images*

Library of Congress Cataloging-in-Publication Data
is on file at the Library of Congress, Washington, D.C.

ISBN: 9780664261450

Most Westminster John Knox Press books are available at special quantity discounts when purchased in bulk by corporations, organizations, and special-interest groups. For more information, please e-mail SpecialSales@wjkbooks .com.

Contents

Acknowledgments

It would be remiss of me to write a book on love without mentioning those who supported and aided me in this work. First and foremost, I want to thank my family, especially my grandmother, who taught me to love the Bible; and my teachers, especially Susan Niditch and Peter Machinist, who taught me how to read and study it. Though they did not play a direct role in the writing of this book, their influence is undoubtedly present.

The biggest help and support came from Kevin Lam. Kevin helped to clarify my thoughts and my writing so that I could complete this book. I would not have been able to write this book on love without his loving help and support.

Caitlin Parsons, a former student-turned-editor, did her usual editing magic on a tight deadline, as did Daniel Braden at Westminster John Knox Press, whose careful reading and editing of the manuscript improved the work. Indeed, various people at WJK were instrumental to the creation of this book. First and foremost, I am grateful to Robert Ratcliff, who approached me about writing this monograph when I was in my first year of teaching at Austin Presbyterian Theological Seminary. Similarly, my former Bible colleague, Bridgett Green, now the Vice President of Publishing and Editorial Director at WJK, has been an important source of support, friendship, and wisdom.

Speaking of colleagues, I am also thankful for the kind and supportive people I work with at Austin Presbyterian Theological Seminary, especially the members of the Bible department, as well as my colleagues in biblical studies, especially Jonathan Kaplan and Brian Doak, both of whom have generously shared with me their writing and research throughout the years. I am also grateful for the sabbatical that the seminary provided, which allowed me to finish this work.

Finally, I want to thank my students, especially those who took my class on love in the Hebrew Bible. Their thought-provoking questions and comments helped shape how I think about love.

Introduction

The Background of Love

"God is love," the writer of 1 John confidently declares. Yet this theologically pleasing statement raises more questions than answers. In saying this, the writer of 1 John does not so much tell us about the nature or identity of God as to address a riddle with another riddle. That is, if God is love, then what is love? And when we turn to this daunting query, we hit an impasse. Can any possible answer adequately explain love? Writers who have written on the subject say no. For example, Diane Ackerman, the author of a book on this topic, states frankly, "Love . . . cannot be measured or mapped."[1] Indeed, she and other writers go further. Considering how a single term, love, is used to refer to myriad things,[2] they state that love cannot even be defined, let alone explained.[3]

Yet this book attempts to do just that—to explain love. Or at least just a tiny sliver of it. In particular, this work looks closely at a handful of stories in the Hebrew Bible that use or center on the Hebrew term and concept *'ahav/'ahev* or *'ahavah*, translated as the verb "to love" or the noun "love," which I will henceforth simply refer to as *ahav*. This word has an unclear etymology,[4] and

---

1. Diane Ackerman, *A Natural History of Love* (New York: Random House, 1994), xvii.

2. Morton Hunt, *The Natural History of Love* (New York: Anchor Books, Doubleday, 1959), 5, 7.

3. Diane Ackerman writes, "Everyone admits that love is wonderful and necessary, yet no one can agree on what it is" (*History of Love*, xvii).

4. Anthony Tambasco, "Love," in *The Collegeville Pastoral Dictionary of Biblical Theology*, ed. Carroll Stuhlmueller (Collegeville: Liturgical Press, 1996), 567–68; Gerhard Wallis, "אהב," in *Theological Dictionary of the Old Testament*, vol. 1, ed. G. Johannes Botterweck and Helmer Ringgren, trans. G. Wallis (Grand Rapids: Eerdmans, 1977), 99–118.

appears at least two hundred times in the Hebrew Bible as a verb[5] and almost fifty times as a noun.[6] Through a close reading of these narratives, this examination, though limited, also explores larger questions concerning love: What does love look like in the Hebrew Bible? What do biblical writers say about love, and more important, what do they mean when they use this term and concept? How is love portrayed, discussed, and conceptualized? What is associated with this term, and what nuances does it have in the Hebrew biblical corpus? Through this research, by offering more insight into this complex and difficult concept, I show that the Hebrew Bible is "as rich a source of insight into love as has ever been put to page,"[7] and is integral to the ways in which relationships, both among people and also between humanity and God, are imagined in the Hebrew text. As a result, an understanding of love in the Hebrew Bible remains fundamental to our knowledge of the biblical text.

BACKGROUND AND PURPOSE OF THIS STUDY

Love is difficult to discuss. Something about this subject induces even the most well-intentioned interpreter to slip into something approaching a bad sermon, aphorism, or pedagogical "lesson." Indeed, I am well-accustomed to sermons and pedagogical lessons. To provide some background, I am a 1.5 generation (or more accurately, 1.75) Korean American woman who received her doctorate in Hebrew Bible. Like in many Korean American families, religion and church were central. My paternal grandmother had converted to Christianity in North Korea before she fled to the South during the Korean War. And she was so pious and dedicated to the church that she pressured my uncle to become a minister when we moved to the United States. I, of course, as a female, was never pushed, never advised to go into religion as a possible career. (However, I was advised to go to law school; so perhaps it was more about money and practicality than gender.)

Looking back, my family's background influenced my interest in the biblical text and my decision to become a scholar of the Bible. And in turn, my background influences how I read these stories and how I understand love in them. For example, the centrality of God and family in the understanding of love in the Hebrew text feels familiar. Also recognizable is the idea that love is intrinsically connected to sacrifice and suffering in the Hebrew Bible; and that

---

5. Katharine Doob Sakenfeld, "Love," in *The Anchor Bible Dictionary,* vol. 4, ed. David Noel Freedman (New York: Doubleday, 1992), 376. Leon Morris says the term appears 208 times (*Testaments of Love: A Study of Love in the Bible* [Grand Rapids: Eerdmans, 1981], 9).

6. Wallis, "אהב," 102.

7. Douglas N. Morgan, "Love in the Hebrew Bible," *Judaism* 5 (1956): 31.

love, while deeply felt, is more often and more clearly demonstrated through behavior and actions than through words.

My background also may explain my longstanding interest in love. Growing up in a family where declarations of love were rare but actions that demonstrated love were frequent, I have long wondered what love really was. I had even originally wanted to examine love in the Hebrew Bible for my dissertation. However, when I mentioned this as a possible topic to an eminent Israeli scholar of the Hebrew Bible more than a decade ago, she rightly steered me away from this topic, stating that it was too complex a subject for the dissertation format. I was still too green, she hinted, to address such a challenging topic, especially while simultaneously trying to satisfy the sometimes sporadic and whimsical concerns of a dissertation committee. She was wise and correct in her guidance, and I wrote my dissertation on a different subject.

Yet when I finally turned to write on this topic a little over a decade after receiving my doctorate, I have not found it easier to write about. I even wondered at times if the senior scholar in Israel had it all wrong. The older I got, the more I realized my limitations. I had much less time, energy, or knowledge than I had hoped and imagined I would have at this age. The goalposts seem to keep moving. Perhaps love is for the young, I dejectedly thought at times while trying to write this book. Maybe this topic is better fit for newer scholars who, with their fresh energy, eager bravado, and less experience, have yet to recognize fully the immensity and complexity of this topic and therefore have the confidence to barge ahead, forcing the biblical text to yield its secrets.

Yet here we are nonetheless, and what you are reading is a book where I attempt to explain a bit more about love in the Hebrew text. Like most things in life, all you can you do is try—especially if you have already agreed to write on this topic with a publisher and have signed a contract. Needless to say, this subject is immensely complicated. Indeed, as I stated earlier, love is tricky because it is difficult to talk about and even more difficult to think about in ways that are not clichéd and hollow. This is especially the case when the topic concerns love in combination with anything having to do with God, such as love in the Hebrew Bible. When working with theologically significant texts and ideas, the temptation to lapse into meaningless truisms or facile advice, such as "God loves the world" or "you should love God," is especially strong.

These easy lapses into tautologies or preachy or teachy sounding nonsense stem from the ambiguity and vastness of love. Love is immensely important, but it is nearly impossible to define and explain because it is used to talk about many different things. This problem is compounded when the subject is not just love, but love in ancient religious texts—texts from way back when, from a non-Western part of the world, and which were handed down, edited, revised, and eventually canonized over a long period of time. The gap between the modern-day interpreter/reader and these stories is so enormous that it feels and may be almost unbridgeable. Indeed, though my identity and context has undoubtedly affected my reading, I am pretty sure that someone like me—a 1.75-generation, female Korean American Bible scholar—was never imagined by the biblical authors, editors, or even modern biblical scholars a mere sixty years ago to be the intended audience, reader, or interpreter of this text.

Yet the very difficulties of understanding love in such a text—the challenges—elucidate the very reason why we should try to understand it better. The gulf between text and reader points to the need. Because we cannot and should not presume that love had the same connotations in the Bible as it does today, more knowledge of love will help us to better understand the biblical text—a text that many of us consider authoritative and religiously significant and meaningful in some way. What does it mean, for example, when it states that "You shall love the LORD" (Deut. 6:5) or that "you shall love your neighbor as yourself" (Lev. 19:18)? Indeed, we cannot presume to understand even simple statements in the Bible such as "Jacob loved Rachel" (Gen. 29:18) without really knowing what love means in this particular story.

Relatedly, better comprehension of the connotations of love in the Hebrew Bible will help us from lapsing into stereotypes and generalities, especially about the Bible and the people from which this text stems. For example, it is not uncommon for people I meet in adult Sunday school or sometimes in my classes to wonder aloud to me in a fit of quasi- or perhaps full Marcionite longing whether it would have been and perhaps still would be best to simply drop the first part of the Bible and, along with it, the supposedly "unfriendly," "not-so-loving," "foreign" deity so prominently featured in it. If not drop, they hint, maybe it would be better to simply skip this first half of the Bible or pretend it does not exist,[8] and instead focus on the second portion, the place where the "friendlier" and "more familiar" God, the one who actually loves and cares, is found. This tendency to privilege the New Testament (and by extension, to center Christianity over against Judaism) as the only part of the canon that speaks about love and, therefore, the "nicer" or more relevant testament stems, in part, from our ignorance of the place of love in the Hebrew corpus.

Moreover, aside from greater literary and theological comprehension, a better understanding of love in the Hebrew biblical text also has some practical and personal benefits. Though this is not a pastoral book, greater knowledge of the Hebrew text and what it says about love can be personally meaningful, especially if the reader views the biblical text as authoritative in some way. As

---

8. On the difficulty of ascertaining a Christian theology of the Old Testament, see Jon D. Levenson, *The Hebrew Bible, The Old Testament and Historical Criticism: Jews and Christians in Biblical Studies* (Louisville: Westminster John Knox, 2012), esp. 62–81.

the biblical scholar Jacqueline Lapsley puts it, understanding what love means in the Hebrew text is fundamental if we are to grasp how God loves humans and how we, in turn, are to love God.[9] Moreover, better comprehension of the various ways that different ancient writers, especially biblical writers, conceived of love will help increase our knowledge of love in general. Indeed, the personal and practical implications of this understanding cannot be overstated according to bell hooks. As she wisely notes, "To love well is the task in all meaningful relationships, not just romantic bonds."[10]

CONTOURS OF THIS STUDY

In the chapters that follow, I hope to further our understanding of love by presenting a theological and literary examination of love in the Hebrew Bible. As Lapsley insightfully observes, a study of love "is not simply a matter of examining specific occurrences of the terms for love," but how the narrative framework of certain stories "shapes how love is conceived."[11] As such, considering the importance of narrative framework, this study focuses on a handful of stories, mostly from the Pentateuch or the Torah (that is the first five books of the Hebrew Bible or the books from Genesis to Deuteronomy), and the Deuteronomistic History (that is, the books of Joshua, Judges, 1 and 2 Samuel, and 1 and 2 Kings), that use or mention *ahav*. For those familiar with the general layout of the Hebrew Bible, I have focused on the narrative portion of the Hebrew text. Though I do briefly discuss the Song of Songs in the final chapter of this work, this means that I largely leave aside the rich but very complicated poetic and prophetic portions (known as the Latter Prophets or the Minor and Major Prophets) of the Hebrew Scriptures that mention *ahav*.

Moreover, to further narrow this vast subject into something more manageable, I have limited my focus to the term *ahav* and the stories that mention or use this term. There are certainly other important terms and concepts that are related to and perhaps even overlap with *ahav*, such as *sana'*, which means "hate," or *hesed*, a multivalent word, which has a range of connotations but is usually translated as "loving kindness" or "loyalty" or "steadfast love."[12] However, in this study, I stick to just this one term and concept, *ahav*, and the stories

9. Jacqueline Lapsley, "Feeling Our Way: Love for God in Deuteronomy," *Catholic Biblical Quarterly* 65, no. 3 (2003): 350–69, esp. 366–69.

10. bell hooks, *All About Love: New Visions* (New York: William Morrow & Company, 2001), 9.

11. Lapsley, "Feeling Our Way," 355.

12. See, e. g., Nelson Glueck, *Hesed in the Bible*, trans. A. Gottschalk (Cincinnati: The Hebrew Union College Press, 1967); Katharine Doob Sakenfeld, *The Meaning of Hesed in the Hebrew Bible: A New Inquiry* (Missoula: Scholars Press, 1978); Glenn Yarbrough, "The Significance of *hsd* in the Old Testament" (PhD diss., Southern Baptist Theological Seminary, 1959).

that use or prominently feature it. A study of *ahav* is challenging enough without the need to add in other equally dense terms and concepts. Speaking of terminology, throughout this work, I refer to God by the male pronoun. Not only is God portrayed as male deity throughout the Hebrew corpus, but as I will argue in the last chapter, God's gender impacts how we understand love.

While I focus on *ahav*, this work is not a word study: that is, this book does not consist of a philological examination and classification of *ahav* per se but of a theological and literary analysis of biblical narratives that feature ideas and concepts concerning *ahav*. While word studies are helpful and useful, and though this research has benefited from them, they are mainly of interest to academic specialists. By focusing on the stories instead—stories that I discuss and question in my classes and in my own research—by approaching this topic in a larger, more literary manner, I hope to engage a broader audience. Relatedly, though this research is textually focused, I have tried to keep overly academic jargon, technicalities, and terminology to a minimum.

For those diehard biblical studies fans who are interested in a philological study of *ahav*, there is a useful dissertation on this subject by Alexander To Ha Luc.[13] In his work, Luc examines every occurrence of *ahav* in the Hebrew Bible as well as related synonyms. Moreover, he helpfully categorizes the ways in which the term appears and is utilized in the biblical text. I will discuss Luc's findings a bit more in the first chapter when I go over the history of scholarship on love in the Hebrew Bible. Suffice it to say, however, unlike Luc's dissertation and other words studies, which usually proceed by examining the various occurrences of this word in the biblical text, this work will take a broader perspective, focusing on specific stories about love instead of the ways in which a particular terminology is utilized.

OUTLINE OF THE BOOK

Through this broader exploration of key narratives that contain *ahav*, I will uncover some interesting aspects of love and how it was imagined in the Hebrew text. Among other things, I hope to show that:

> Biblical characters, like people today, more often love those who act like them.
> When it comes to love, there is no separation between actions and emotions.

---

13. Alexander To Ha Luc, "The Meaning of *'hb* in the Hebrew Bible" (PhD diss. University of Wisconsin–Madison, 1982). For a brief discussion on the meanings of *ahav*, see also Ellen van Wolde, *Reframing Biblical Studies: When Language and Text Meet Culture, Cognition, and Context* (Winona Lake: Eisenbrauns, 2009), 45–50.

Love is associated with food and the enjoyment of it but not in an altogether positive manner.

There are distinctions made between love based on appetites and bodies and a love that is higher and divine.

Love in the Hebrew text is deeply intertwined with the matters of politics and power.

Love is connected to divine preference and favoritism, and also its opposite, divine rejection.

Love is envisioned as mysterious and unknowable and perhaps even capricious as a result of its connection to God.

Though God's preferences are connected to love, God is also vulnerable to love's powers and is capable of heartbreak and blindness when it comes to the object of his love.

Love has a gendered meaning, as female characters are almost never said to be the ones who love and also experience the negative effects of love more so in the Hebrew text.

The negative association between love and women, however, might indicate that love is a feminine force.

Therefore, love in the Hebrew Bible, as in life, remains complicated, contradictory, and ultimately mysterious, and therefore a key source of questions and struggles.

Despite these complexities, love is a vital component of the ideology and theology of the Hebrew Scriptures, and therefore an understanding of it remains fundamental to our knowledge of the biblical text.

To see the ways in which these messages and meanings about love emerge and are reflected in these stories, I begin our exploration of love in the first chapter by going over briefly the history of scholarship on this subject. Though I have tried to keep this book readable and geared toward a nonspecialist audience, some foray into the academic research on this topic is unavoidable, yet, I hope, helpful. That is, in order to know how this work stems from, veers from, and adds to previous understandings of love in the Hebrew Bible, we have to know what others have said on this topic. Hence, in the first chapter, I summarize quickly what we know thus far about love in the Hebrew biblical text. In particular, this chapter discusses the general scholarly consensus that the covenant between God and Israel, as facilitated by Moses, plays a key role in the conception and understanding of love in the Hebrew Bible. This love, known as covenantal love, has theological, familial, social, political, and emotional valences, which bleed into other instances where *ahav* is mentioned. Hence, the covenantal understanding of love is evident in and indeed affects the meaning of other stories about love in the Hebrew corpus.

Moving from the covenant between God and his people, the second chapter highlights the divinity of love by examining the story of Rebekah and Isaac, and their twin sons, Jacob and Esau. Rebekah loves one twin, Jacob, while

Isaac loves the other twin, Esau (Gen. 25:28). The oppositional parental love of their children divides love into two types: a higher, holy kind of love, and a baser, more appetite-centered love. Though the narrative asserts the divinity and superiority of this higher love, it also simultaneously undermines this claim of its preeminence by showing how this love leads to deceit, discord, and the disintegration of the family. Through assertion and subversion, the narrative wrestles with love and God's relationship to it.

The power of love is given greater emphasis in the story of Saul and David, the subject of chapter 3. Showing how human love preferences are intimately connected to and indeed mirror divine preferences, this chapter explores the ramifications of divine favoritism and its opposite, divine rejection, on love. Similar to Esau and Jacob, Saul, the divinely rejected, is contrasted to David, the divinely favored. As a result of God's preferences, David becomes increasingly beloved by everyone around him, while Saul, in contrast, becomes increasingly unloved. This, in turn, leads to a decrease in success and political power for Saul and an opposing rise in power and prestige for David. Despite the dramatic effects of divine favoritism and rejection, the narrative never explains the reason behind God's capricious preferences. However, clues in the story suggest that God's rejection of Saul results from divine heartbreak and that God too is vulnerable to love's powers.

Continuing the exploration of love in the stories about David and Saul in chapter 4, I turn to the painful effects of divine favoritism and rejection on Saul's family, especially Saul's firstborn son, Jonathan. Looking at the various interpretations of David and Jonathan's love relationship, one which some have argued is erotic or romantic, this chapter uncovers the betrayals that mark their relationship as well as that between Jonathan and his father. These betrayals are explained and downplayed by the biblical authors in two ways: by contrasting the unfavored, unloved, and ungifted Saul to the favored, respected, and gifted doubles, Jonathan and David; and by using love to obscure David's role in using these betrayals to usurp Saul's throne. The problematic portrayal of God as supportive of David's exploitation of the love of Jonathan and Saul hints that God too might be enamored of David, so much so that he has turned a blind eye to his beloved's ruthless machinations.

In the final chapter, I turn to the relationship between love and gender by focusing on the stories about female characters who are either the active subjects or the passive objects of love. Reflecting discomfort with the connection between love and women, almost all the female characters suffer as a result of their love. Hence, the narrative appears to target women who are associated with love for special punishment. Similar feelings are evident in the ultimate erotic love song in the Hebrew text, the Song of Songs/Solomon, or Canticles. This book, which features a seemingly sexually open and expressive female protagonist, initially seems to celebrate female expressions of love. At the same time, however, by associating the female lover with images of violence, war, and death, the book evinces a deep sense of ambivalence and apprehension about women and their role in love.

In the conclusion, I summarize what we have learned about love in the Hebrew Bible through our exploration and close reading of stories that mention *ahav*. Love, *ahav*, is depicted as a dense term and concept that has a web of associations, meanings, and connections—and it is this dense consortium of meanings that is evoked when *ahav* is used and appears in a particular narrative. In particular, in the stories we have explored, love is shown to be a divine, powerful, painful, mysterious, and ultimately feminine force that might be on par with God. As such, through the use of *ahav*, the biblical writers ultimately profess to both the lingering significance of love as well as its ultimate unknowability and mystery.

1

The Agreement of Love

Love and the Covenant

INTRODUCTION

When I began exploring love in the Hebrew Bible, I was certain that I would encounter a mountain of research. The Hebrew corpus, after all, is part of the canon of two major Abrahamic faiths, Judaism and Christianity. Surely every aspect of it must have been perused and studied, especially a concept as important as love. Yet to my surprise, I found that the topic, for some reason, was less investigated than I assumed. Indeed, Leon Morris, a biblical scholar who has authored one of the few books on the subject, remarks on the dearth of research on this topic. In his monograph on love in the Hebrew Bible, the Septuagint, and the New Testament, Morris wonders how "so many scholars can write so much about the Old Testament with so little formal recognition of the place of love in it."[1]

As I researched a bit more, however, things were not as dire as Morris suggested when he was writing in 1981. In the past couple of years, renowned Hebrew Bible scholar Jon Levenson has published a book on a closely related topic—love of God in the Hebrew Bible and in Judaism.[2] Though Levenson's work, which I will discuss again later in this chapter, is insightful and illuminating, it is not wholly unprecedented. Rather, Morris, because his specialty centered on the New Testament, appears to have been less familiar with

---

1. Leon Morris, *Testaments of Love: A Study of Love in the Bible* (Grand Rapids: Eerdmans, 1981), 4–5.
2. Jon D. Levenson, *The Love of God: Divine Gift, Human Gratitude, and Mutual Faithfulness in Judaism* (Princeton: Princeton University Press, 2020).

scholarship on the Hebrew Bible. Contra his critique, there have indeed been scholars who have recognized the importance of love in the Hebrew corpus. In this chapter, I briefly turn to these scholars and their works.

I realize that the history of scholarship is not usually the most exciting part of a book. Nonetheless, it remains important. As the famous writer and humorist Terry Pratchett says, "If you do not know where you come from, then you don't know where you are, and if you don't know where you are, then you don't know where you're going. And if you don't know where you're going, you're probably going wrong."[3] That is, without knowing what others have said on this topic (where you come from), it is hard to know what contributions are needed on the subject matter (where you are going). As a result, it is difficult to figure out what new things to say about the topic, and whether it is new at all (where you are). In such a case, generalized confusion ensues, thereby greatly increasing the chances of going awry (probably going wrong).

WILLIAM MORAN AND COVENANTAL LOVE

Now that the significance of the history of scholarship has been established, let us return briefly to Leon Morris, who, as I mentioned earlier, bemoaned the lack of research on this topic. Although Morris acknowledges the deficiency in scholarship, his book on love unfortunately does not fill the gap in knowledge that he so helpfully points out. As I mentioned earlier, this likely has to do with his area of expertise, which is not the Hebrew text. Rather, as a scholar of the New Testament, Morris's bias and knowledge lies with a different corpus of text in which, as he puts it, "there is, as we might expect, a greater readiness to see love as significant."[4] As expected, his analysis of love in the Hebrew Bible is sweeping, general, and more homiletical than exegetical.

Had Morris been a scholar of the Hebrew Bible, I hope that he would not have so easily dismissed it as lacking "a readiness to see love as significant."[5] Moreover, had Morris been interested in the Hebrew Scriptures as something more than a sidekick of the New Testament, he would have discussed at length the work of William Moran, an important ancient Near Eastern scholar, instead of relegating his work to a mere footnote. Morris would have done so because he would have realized the significance of Moran's groundbreaking (and succinct) article on love in the Hebrew Bible. This article, though

3. Terry Pratchett, *I Shall Wear Midnight* (New York: HarperCollins, 2010), 351.
4. Morris, *Testaments of Love*, 5.
5. Morris, *Testaments of Love*, 5.

published in 1963,[6] still remains the starting point for almost all scholarship on love in the Hebrew text.

I will explain Moran's article in detail shortly, but a summary of his main points will set the scene for the more comprehensive examination that follows: Moran's central argument is that love in the book of Deuteronomy is mainly a political term associated with treaties. As a result, he posits that love has a particular meaning in Deuteronomy: it is a "covenantal love" or "a love defined by and pledged in the covenant." Covenantal love, according to Moran, is wholly different from "parental or conjugal love," that is, love between parents and children, or between romantic partners. Rather, covenantal love—that is, the love mentioned in Deuteronomy and which forms the center of the relationship between Israel and God—is a "love that can be commanded" and which is "expressed in loyalty, in service, and in unqualified obedience to the demands of the Law."[7] Covenantal love, in short, entails actions: namely obedience to the commandments; and therefore, as interpreters would later come to understand and apply Moran's ideas, love does not necessarily entail emotion or affection.

To see how Moran arrives at his conclusion, we have to understand why he was looking at Deuteronomy, covenants, and treaties—things that initially seem unrelated to love—in the first place. That is, how did Moran come to the conclusion that "if Deuteronomy is the biblical document *par excellence* of love, it is also the biblical document *par excellence* of the covenant."[8] Hence, in order to fully appreciate and comprehend Moran's argument, which, in turn, is needed in order to understand what love means in the Hebrew Bible, we need to examine briefly the history of scholarship on Deuteronomy as well as covenants and treaties; and we also need to explore how covenants, especially the one described in Deuteronomy, pertains to love.

DEUTERONOMY, LOVE, AND COVENANTS

There are many covenants (*berit* in Hebrew) in the Hebrew Bible, but the covenant that is pertinent to our discussion is the one that God makes with Moses and the people of Israel after the exodus from Egypt, which is recounted in the book of Deuteronomy.[9] The appearance of the covenant

---

6. William Moran, "The Ancient Near Eastern Background of the Love of God in Deuteronomy," *Catholic Biblical Quarterly* 25, no. 1 (1963): 77–87, here 78.

7. Moran, "Ancient Near Eastern Background," 78.

8. Moran, "Ancient Near Eastern Background," 82.

9. George E. Mendenhall and Gary A. Herion define covenant as "an agreement enacted between two parties in which one or both make promises under oath to perform or refrain

in Deuteronomy is in part the reason why Moran focuses on this book in his article on love. Deuteronomy is important to the study of love because the book frequently uses the Hebrew term for "love" or "to love"—'*ahavah* or '*ahav*/'*ahev*, respectively—which comes from the Hebrew root aleph-heh-bet (the bet is pronounced either as "b" or "v"). (For the sake of simplicity and clarity, I will, henceforth, refer to both the verb and the noun as *ahav*.[10]) As we will see, it is not a coincidence that Deuteronomy frequently uses *ahav*. Rather, it is precisely because Deuteronomy contains a covenant that it so often mentions love.

Framed as a series of speeches given by Moses to the Israelites on the plains of Moab at the end of their desert wandering and before their entrance into the promised land, that is, the land of Canaan, Deuteronomy is the last book of a section of the Hebrew Bible known as the Torah or the Pentateuch. The name of the book, Deuteronomy, from the Greek *deuteros*, "second," and *nomos*, "law," means "the second law."[11] And the title hints of the book's contents. That is, at the center of Deuteronomy, as part of the speeches, is an exposition of God's laws or commandments, referred to as the Deuteronomic Code (Deut. 12–26). The Deuteronomic Code makes up a significant part of the covenant between God and Israel.

Though Deuteronomy has been robustly examined by scholars because of its importance to the compositional and editorial history of the Hebrew Bible, it has been largely ignored by general readers of the Bible. This disregard, in part, stems from Deuteronomy's focus on the laws—that is, commandments given by God to the people of Israel—which many, especially Christian readers, dismiss as uninteresting and irrelevant. This misbelief stems from and is compounded by a particular confusion. Namely, though covenants are esteemed by many as religiously significant, many are unaware that a covenant, especially the one between Israel and God, is in fact based on a contract or treaty—one which, predictably, is filled with stipulations. In the Hebrew text, these stipulations are expressed as God's laws and commandments.[12]

---

from certain actions stipulated in advance" ("Covenant," in *Anchor Bible Dictionary*, vol. 1, ed. David Noel Freedman [New York: Doubleday, 1992], 1179–1202 [1179]).

10. Either the verb or the noun form of *ahav* occur in Deuteronomy at 4:37; 5:10; 6:5; 7:8, 9, 13; 10:12, 15, 18, 19; 11:1, 13, 22; 13:3; 15:16; 19:9; 21:15, 16; 23:5; and 30:6, 16, 20.

11. This understanding of Deuteronomy is echoed in rabbinic texts, which refer to this book as the *mishneh torah*, or the "second teaching," or "the second instruction," a designation that stems from Deut. 17:18, which talks about how a king of Israel should make for himself a *mishneh torah*, "a copy of this law," so that he can study and revere it.

12. Jon Levenson writes that this replacement of stipulations with laws and commandments—that is, "the placement of law within a covenantal framework"—is unparalleled and "momentous" in so far as it "means that the observance even of humdrum matters of law has become an expression of personal faithfulness and loyalty in the covenant" (*Love of God*, 14).

These so-called "irrelevant" things called laws or commandments, such as those found in the Deuteronomic Code, are, in short, fundamental aspects of what constitute a covenant, which is itself a kind of treaty or agreement.

This idea that Deuteronomy, or at least parts of Deuteronomy (as well as parts of Exodus, which also entails a covenant between God and Israel called the "Book of the Covenant" or the Covenant Code [Exod. 20:22–23:19]), sound a lot like treaties, and indeed, may consist of one, stems from a series of discoveries. In the early twentieth century, archaeologists uncovered a vast number of treaties from the first and second millennium (that is, the Late Bronze and Early Iron Age) from an ancient people in Anatolia and Syria called the Hittites, spurring on the study of these documents. The Amarna Letters (c. 1400–1350 BCE),[13] an archive of diplomatic correspondences between the Egyptian Pharoah and the various regional leaders of Canaan and nearby states, gives a peek into the nature of international relationships a couple of centuries later. During this period, the areas that encompassed and surrounded Israel were made up of numerous small kingdoms. These kingdoms, unfortunately, were situated between two superpowers, Egypt and Mesopotamia, which battled for control over this important region. As a result, this area was a hotbed of political wheelings and dealings—and therefore an area much accustomed to political agreements. As a result, many treaties were made and utilized; and therefore, as a result of their ubiquity, the language, ideas, and concepts found in these treaties were widely prevalent throughout the ancient Near East—so much so that they would have been picked up by those in ancient Israel, including those who might have been responsible for the writing of the Hebrew Scriptures.

When these treaties from the ancient Near East were discovered, scholars naturally started reading them and comparing them to the Hebrew Bible. And when they did, they found that these treaties curiously sounded similar to parts of the Hebrew text. In particular, the covenants made by God and Israel, which are described in the books of Exodus and Deuteronomy, appeared to resemble the outline of these ancient agreements. Take, for example, the general structure of an ancient Near Eastern suzerain-vassal treaty: (1) preamble, which names and gives the titles of the more powerful party and also recounts the relationship history of the parties (historical prologue), usually the times when the more powerful party came to the defense or rescue of the weaker party; (2) stipulations, that is, the expectations and obligations of the treaty; (3) provisions for depositing a copy of the treaty in the temple and periodic reading of the agreement; (4) witnesses, usually gods or natural elements, such as

13. Found in 1887 CE, the Amarna Letters helped scholars get an in-depth sense of the political situation and international diplomacy in the region during that period.

the sun, mountains, winds, and so on; and (5) blessings and curses, which lists the benefits of obedience and the consequences of disobedience.

Compare the outline of these treaties with the covenant given by God to the Israelites in the books of Deuteronomy and Exodus: (1) preamble with the name and title of the more powerful party—"I am the LORD your God . . ." (Exod. 20:2a; Deut. 5:6a), as well as a recounting of the relationship history of the parties—". . . who brought you out of the land of Egypt, out of the house of slavery" (Exod. 20:2b; Deut. 5:6b [cf. Deut. 1–3]);[14] (2) stipulations, that is, the expectations and obligations of the treaty expressed as laws/commandments, beginning with, "You shall have no other gods before me . . ." (Exod. 20:3–17; Deut. 5:7–21 [cf. Deut. 12–26]); (3) the command to archive and deposit (Exod. 25:21; cf. Exod. 40:20; Deut. 10:5) and periodically review the covenant (Deut. 31:10–12; cf. Exod. 24:7; Josh. 8:30–35); (4) witnesses (Deut. 4:26; 30:19–20; 31:28); and finally (5) blessings and curses (Deut. 27:11–28:68), and the notice that this covenant was ratified (Exod. 24:3–8).[15]

The parallels between the covenants in Deuteronomy and Exodus, and ancient Near Eastern treaties were undoubtable. Indeed, "the Mosaic covenant" appeared to be "structured upon the same literary and ideological foundations as were the secular treaties."[16] So similar were the two that scholars even proposed that covenants may indeed have originated from these treaties.[17] Hence, one of the most significant and sacred institutions in the Bible—the covenant—likely had secular and non-Israelite origins.[18]

The affinities between ancient Near Eastern agreements and the covenants in the Hebrew text did not end there. Scholars also realized that covenants sounded weirdly similar to treaties as well. And this brings us back again to Moran and his argument. This comparison of covenants in the Hebrew Bible, especially Deuteronomy, with other ancient Near Eastern treaties led scholars

---

14. All translations of the Bible, unless otherwise marked, are from the NRSV.

15. Sandra L. Richter, *Epic of Eden: A Christian Entry into the Old Testament* (Downers Grove: IVP Academic, 2008), 79–88; Jon D. Levenson, *Sinai and Zion: An Entry into the Jewish Bible* (San Francisco: HarperSanFrancisco, 1985), 26–36; Kenton L. Sparks, *Ancient Texts for the Study of the Hebrew Bible: A Guide to the Background Literature* (Grand Rapids: Baker Academic, 2017), 435–48.

16. Richter, *Epic of Eden*, 63.

17. George E. Mendenhall, "Covenant Forms in Israelite Tradition," *Biblical Archaeologist* 17, no. 3 (1954): 50–76, esp. 55–57; Mendenhall, *Law and Covenant in Israel and the Ancient Near East* (Pittsburg: Biblical Colloquium, 1955), 10.

18. Once scholars realized the covenants mimicked treaties, or that covenants might be treaties, this led to the discovery of other parallels. For example, prominent Israeli scholar Moshe Weinfeld argued that the covenant God made with Abraham and David should be understood as a particular kind of suzerain-vassal agreement, which he calls the promissory type. These covenants, he argued, were modeled on the "royal grant" and centered on gifts of land and dynasty bestowed upon an individual by a lord for loyal service ("The Covenant of Grant in the Old Testament and in the Ancient Near East," *Journal of the American Oriental Society* 90, no. 2 [1970]: 184–203).

to rethink the language, terminology, and concepts used in covenants, especially *ahav*, or love. In particular, Moran noticed that God's frequent commands to the Israelites to love God in Deuteronomy (Deut. 6:5; 10:12; 11:1, 13, 22; 13:3; 19:9; 30:16, 20) would be strange if love were thought of as an emotion, which was how love was considered in 1963 when Moran was writing his article and largely how it is still considered today. If love were an emotion, how could God demand that the Israelites feel a certain way toward God or other people? Unlike actions, the assumption was that emotions could not be commanded. Hence, Moran posited that love must have had a different meaning in the Hebrew text from the emotional meaning ascribed to it in modern times.

Going further, Moran found that, in Deuteronomy, *ahav* was frequently found in and intertwined with the covenant described in the book. That is, the command to love was usually mentioned in covenants or, as he puts it, this kind of love was "a love defined by and pledged in the covenant," and that it seemed "intimately related to fear and reverence." As such, Moran concluded that what was meant by love, especially in Deuteronomy, was a "covenantal love." That is, unlike how we conceive of love now—as an internal feeling and emotion often linked to romance—love in Deuteronomy was imagined differently. *Ahav*, according to Moran, instead mainly entailed actions, in particular "loyalty" and "unqualified obedience to the demands of the Law." And, as such, it was "a love that can be commanded."[19]

Coming back to treaties, Moran suggested that this concept of "covenantal love" in Deuteronomy was not a wholly new idea but came from elsewhere.[20] And this "elsewhere," Moran argued, were other ancient Near Eastern treaties, which also utilized terminology and concepts that sounded and meant something very similar to covenantal love. In particular, the use and meaning of love in the covenant in Deuteronomy seemed to particularly align with those found in a type of treaty called the suzerain-vassal treaty, so named because it was a treaty made between a more powerful entity, the lord or suzerain, and a less powerful entity, the vassal. Like in Deuteronomy, these ancient Near Eastern suzerain-vassal treaties also demanded that the vassals love their suzerain and therefore also used love to connote loyalty, service, and obedience. For example, in a seventh-century treaty from Assyria, an ancient state in Mesopotamia, a vassal swears the following: "(You swear) that you will love Ashurbanipal, the crown-prince, son of Esarhaddon, king of Assyrian, your lord as (you do) yourselves (or your life)."[21] In another document, a vassal

19. Moran, "Ancient Near Eastern Background," 78.
20. Moran, "Ancient Near Eastern Background," 77–78.
21. D. J. Wiseman, "The Vassal-Treaties of Esarhaddon," *Iraq* 20, no. 1 (1958): i–ii, 1–99 (78).

states: "Ashurbanipal, king of Assyria, our lord, we love [. . .] and another king and another lord for . . . we shall never seek."[22] The similarity between these treaty statements and the well-known command in Deuteronomy to "love the LORD your God with all your heart, and with all your soul, and with all your might" (Deut. 6:5) is striking. The two seem to use and conceive of love in the same way.

These similarities led Moran to conclude that the particular type of "pro-fane" love evinced in Deuteronomy—covenantal love—must have been influenced by these other ancient Near Eastern documents. As such, Moran concluded that love in Hebrew text, especially Deuteronomy, as in ancient Near Eastern treaties, was a political or legal term connoting political loyalty, service, and obedience. Love entailed action—actions that indicated fidelity to the treaty or covenant; and as such, it was a love that could be demanded or ordered.

ACTIONS, EMOTIONS, AND COVENANTAL LOVE

Moran's conclusion that love was a political term that entailed actions, in particular those that expressed fidelity to a covenant or treaty, was widely applied. A quick summary of some scholars and their works, some of which we will discuss in more detail in subsequent chapters, shows the extent of Moran's influence. For example, in his momentous work on Deuteronomy, the Hebrew Bible scholar Moshe Weinfeld, following Moran, argues that love connotes "religious loyalty."[23] Gerhard Wallis, another biblical scholar, concurs, arguing that the command in Deuteronomy that Israel was to love God did "not in the original sense" entail "emotion," but instead "genuine obedience and pure devotion."[24] Along similar lines, J. W. McKay builds on Dennis McCarthy's claim that the relationship between YHWH and Israel is like that between father and son, a metaphor that Moran thought was absent in Deuteronomy.[25] McKay posits that the famous statement in Deuteronomy 6:5—"You shall love the LORD your God with all your heart, and with all your soul, and with all your might"—which forms part of the Shema, the Jewish confession of faith, does not entail an emotional sentiment but rather that of

22. Leroy Waterman, *Royal Correspondence of the Assyrian Empire* (Ann Arbor: University of Michigan Press, 1930–36), 267.

23. Moshe Weinfeld, *Deuteronomy and the Deuteronomic School* (Oxford: Clarendon, 1972), 84.

24. Gerhard Wallis, "אהב," in *Theological Dictionary of the Old Testament*, eds. G. Johannes Botterweck and Helmer Ringgren, vol. 1 (Grand Rapids: Eerdmans, 1977), 99–18, esp. 115.

25. Dennis J. McCarthy, "Notes on the Love of God in Deuteronomy and the Father-Son Relationship between Yahweh and Israel," *Catholic Biblical Quarterly* 27, no. 2 (1965): 144–47.

"*pietas*, the filial love and obedience that the son offers to the *pater familias*," which thus can be commanded.[26]

So influential was Moran's argument that other scholars also started applying his conclusions to other parts of the Hebrew Bible outside Deuteronomy, something which Moran did to some degree as well.[27] J. A. Thompson and Katharine Doob Sakenfeld, for example, spell out the covenantal meanings of love evinced in other biblical narratives, such as that of the relationship between David and Jonathan.[28] Moreover, Susan Ackerman notes the odd lack of the use of *ahav* to describe feelings that women have of men or to describe feelings children have of their parents. She concludes that there was some overlap between the way that love is used to describe interpersonal relationships and the connotation it has in the covenant in Deuteronomy where *ahav* is usually used to convey how a "hierarchically superior party" feels about the lesser party.[29]

Other commentators, while agreeing with the broad contours of Moran's conclusion, have tried to modify and refine it. In particular, some have questioned whether the bifurcation between action and emotion, which was assumed by Moran and which comes to be more fully enunciated by later scholars influenced by his work, reflects an underlying Christian bias.[30] That is, Moran's idea that love in the Hebrew text is centered on actions—namely, obedience to the commandments of the covenant—and not necessarily on emotion can be seen as suggestive of the old Christian charge that Jews are overly legalistic or focused on the law.[31] Reflected in this is the assumption that the works and law of the Old Testament have been surpassed and

26. J. W. McKay, "Man's Love for God in Deuteronomy and the Father/Teacher-Son/ Pupil Relationship," *Vetus Testamentum* 22, fasc. 4 (1972): 432.

27. Moran also suggests that the political connotation of love extends outside of Deuteronomy. For example, 1 Kgs. 5:1, which talks about the covenant between Solomon, the king of Judah and Israel, and Hiram, the king of Tyre, calls Hiram a lover (*'ohev*) of King David. Moreover Joab, David's general, tells David, who is grieving the death of his rebellious son Absalom, to stop "hating those who love you (*'ohaveka*)" in 2 Sam. 19:6. These references to love only make sense if love and lovers refer to those bound by legal or political allegiances of a treaty or covenant—that is, if it referred to allies—and if love concerned a covenantal love ("Ancient Near Eastern Background," 80–81).

28. J. A. Thompson, "The Significance of the Verb *Love* in the David-Jonathan Narratives in 1 Samuel," *Vetus Testamentum* 24, fasc. 3 (1974): 334–38; Katharine Doob Sakenfeld, "Loyalty and Love: The Language of Human Interconnections in the Hebrew Bible," *Michigan Quarterly Review* 22, no. 3 (1983): 190–204. See also P. R. Ackroyd, "The Verb Love—*'aheb* in the David Jonathan Narratives—A Footnote," *Vetus Testamentum* 25 (1975): 213–14.

29. Susan Ackerman, "The Personal Is Political: Covenantal and Affectionate Love (*'aheb, 'ahaba*) in the Hebrew Bible," *Vetus Testamentum* 52, fasc. 4 (2002): 437–56.

30. Jacqueline Lapsley, "Feeling Our Way: Love for God in Deuteronomy," *Catholic Biblical Quarterly* 65, no. 3 (2003): 350–69.

31. See also Lapsley, "Feeling Our Way," 365.

superseded by the emotion- and belief-centric faith of the New Testament. Moran's conclusions, in short, especially the ways they were understood and applied, could be said to follow the tendency in Christian scholarship "to characterize the Jewish scriptures . . . as a set of overly punctilious behavioral norms that operate independent of any higher spiritual correlates."[32]

Scholars of late, therefore, while adopting Moran's core arguments, have attempted to nuance his conclusions by noting that there is no clear and neat division between emotion and action, as Moran might have assumed. An emotion, Moran presupposed, could not be commanded because only actions can be commanded, and a thing was either an emotion or an action but not both. Not only does this assumption seem particularly modern and Western—that is, culturally specific[33]—but this binarism is absent in the religion that more directly arises from the Hebrew text, namely Judaism.

Though these religions are complicated, Judaism seems to be much more comfortable with the idea that emotions and actions are coterminous or tangled up together than is Christianity. As the great Jewish theologian and rabbi Abraham Joshua Heschel writes, "The dichotomy of faith and works which presented such an important problem in Christian theology was never a problem in Judaism. . . . Deed and thought are bound into one. All a person thinks and feels enters everything he does, and all he does is involved in everything he thinks and feels."[34] Indeed, according to well-known and prolific scholar of Judaism Jacob Neusner, Jewish writings, such as the Tosefta, have no qualms about commanding a person to control or change their emotions. Emotions in Judaism, he argues, are seen not as spontaneous but as an aspect of a person's judgment, and as such, they too can be holy or profane. Hence, in Judaism, "our task as human beings demands that we sanctify our emotions as much as carry out actions of holiness."[35]

Modern scholars of the Bible have also come around to similar conclusions and have tried to put emotions back into the idea of love in the Hebrew Bible. Concluding that Moran focused almost exclusively on conduct,[36] commenta-

---

32. Gary A. Anderson, *A Time to Mourn, A Time to Dance: The Expression of Grief and Joy in Israelite Religion* (University Park: Pennsylvania State University Press, 1991), 12, 54.

33. Jacqueline Lapsley writes: "As some historians of love argue, love is something culturally and socially constructed, and thus its 'content' is subject to change. We moderns tend to privatize emotions including love, creating a discrete category of feeling (as distinct from action) to which we assign love" ("Feeling Our Way," 354).

34. Abraham Joshua Heschel, *God in Search of Man: A Philosophy of Judaism* (New York: Farrar, Straus and Giroux, 1983), 296.

35. Jacob Neusner, "The Virtues of the Inner Life in Formative Judaism," *Tikkun* 1, no. 1 (1986): 72–83, esp. 72 and 73.

36. R. W. L. Moberly, "Toward an Interpretation of the Shema," in *Theological Exegesis: Essays in Honor of Brevard S. Childs*, ed. Christopher R. Seitz and Kathryn Greene-McCreight (Grand Rapids: Eerdmans, 1999), 124–44, esp. 134n19.

tors, such as Walter Brueggemann, argue that just because love in the Bible has a political dimension, it does not necessarily "rule out an affective dimension" to it.[37] Bill Arnold echoes Brueggemann when he states that Moran's argument reduces and strips "love" in Deuteronomy of "all affection reducing it only to a cognitive impulse."[38] Love for God in Deuteronomy, he argues, "is certainly more than affection, but not less than affection," and thus the love command is not only a demand for covenant fidelity but also entails an emotional aspect.[39] Indeed, Jacqueline Lapsley states that a vision of love that excludes affection and emotion takes away something essential from the idea of humans loving God and God loving humans. She notes that "Moran and others speak of covenantal love as 'loyalty,' but they strip that loyalty of affect, whereas loyalty can, and often does, have a very strong affective quality."[40] Both are bound up together, she argues.

In the newest monograph on the love of God, Jon Levenson, a well-known scholar of the Hebrew Bible and Judaism, presents one of the fullest explications of how love in the Hebrew Bible entails both action and emotion. Like others I have cited, Levenson also argues that action and emotion cannot really be separated because they are intertwined and mutually influential. He writes that it is not just emotions that generate action, as is usually assumed, but also the reverse: that emotion arises out of action.[41] As such, love indeed can be commanded because it entails action, which itself is not disconnected from emotion, and can indeed cause "the emotion, if that is what love should be called" to "be generated."[42]

Relatedly, Levenson's rich discussion elucidates how odd it is to assume that actions and emotions are discrete and independent of each other. This assumption is especially strange, Levenson seems to suggest, in the case of the love relationship between Israel and God, the drama, passion, and ups-and-downs of which are evident in the Hebrew text. Why assume there are no affections or emotion involved in the love relationship between God and Israel—both Israel's adherence to God's commandments (Israel's love of God) and God's election and choice of Israel (God's love of Israel)—simply because

---

37. Walter Brueggemann, *Theology of the Old Testament: Testimony, Dispute, Advocacy* (Minneapolis: Fortress, 1997), 420; see also 416–17.

38. Bill T. Arnold, "The Love-Fear Antinomy in Deuteronomy 5–11," *Vetus Testamentum* 61, fasc. 4 (2011): 561.

39. Arnold, "The Love-Fear Antinomy," 560.

40. Lapsley, "Feeling Our Way," 354.

41. Levenson writes, "as is well known among social psychologists, behaviors can generate and define emotion" (Levenson, *Love of God*, 32). So also as Gary Anderson states in his work on ritual, grief, and joy, "inner experiences of religious believers are generated by the external forms of their religious tradition" (Anderson, *A Time to Mourn, A Time to Dance*, 7).

42. Levenson, *Love of God*, 32.

the two parties have made a covenant that entails obligations and actions? This strange assumption only makes some sense if it is presumed that Israel follows God's commandments wholly unwillingly or simply by rote or out of fear.[43] That is, Israel does not truly feel anything toward God but is merely going through the motions for some reason. Even if this were the case, however, emotions, albeit negative ones, would likely be present. More important, this assumption leaves little room for the possibility that Israel's obedience stems from willingness and feelings, indeed positive ones, such as a sense of reverence, awe, and love of God and tradition.

Moreover, even if it were the case that love only equals action and that Israel only loved God—that is, went through the motions of obedience—because it was compelled to, this would fail to explain God's love of Israel. God's selection of and love for Israel—the reason why God approaches Israel to make a covenant—as the biblical text states, does not stem from obligation, coercion, or need but is something freely and graciously given (Deut. 7:6–8; 23:5). How can such an act of divine grace have nothing to do with feelings or affection? It is nearly impossible to imagine any love relationship, but especially the one between God and God's people, as devoid of emotion. It is equally difficult to imagine such a love relationship as devoid of action. When it comes to love, most of us naturally assume that emotion and action are not opposites but interconnected partners.

THE COMPLEX MEANING OF LOVE

Nowadays, interpreters assert a richer understanding of love in the Hebrew Bible. Special credit must be given to Alexander To Ha Luc. In his 1982 dissertation, which examines all occurrences of *ahav* and related synonyms in the Hebrew Bible, he already notes that love in the Hebrew text entails both emotion and actions: ". . . the author of Deuteronomy has set a high demand on the practice of religion: genuine inner feeling must go hand in hand with outward observance, loyalty to God must involve both."[44]

Not bound to a discussion of covenantal love, Luc moreover goes further and elucidates the wide range of meaning *ahav* has in the Hebrew Scriptures. Looking at the use of *ahav* in the descriptions of various relationships, such as between parent and child and husband and wife, Luc notes that love can connote intense desire or sexual attraction such as in the Song of Songs (1:7;

43. On love and fear, see Levenson, *Love of God*, 29–36, 59–68.
44. Alexander To Ha Luc, "The Meaning of *'hb* in the Hebrew Bible" (PhD diss., University of Wisconsin-Madison, 1982), 139.

3:1–4) or, more disturbingly, in the narratives about the rape of Dinah (Gen. 34) and that of Tamar (2 Sam. 13). Love also has resonances of romantic feelings and longing as in the case of Jacob and Rachel (Gen. 29). It can also indicate something like preference, as *ahav* is used to describe how the Persian king feels of Esther (Esth. 2:17); Rehoboam of his wife Maacah (2 Chr. 11:21); Jacob of Rachel (Gen. 29:30); Isaac of Esau; and Rebekah of Jacob (Gen. 25:28). In prophetic and wisdom text, *ahav* might even stand for the physical act of lovemaking (Prov. 5:19; Jer. 2:33).[45]

In a similar vein, though what follows is not a word study, I too try to elucidate the rich and complicated matrices of meanings and associations that love has in the Hebrew Bible. As I noted in the introduction, this work shows that love is multivalent, having theological, political, familial, social, and emotional valences. Most importantly—and the purpose of the brief foray into the history of scholarship—the reason why love has these different meanings, I assert, is because of the use and presence of *ahav* in covenants in the Hebrew text. That is, the various meanings and associations that *ahav* has in covenants seep into other instances where *ahav* is used, even in narratives that are not centrally about covenants. As such, Moran's argument about the importance of covenants to an understanding of love, though in need of some modification and adjustment, largely remains true. Love, as expressed, used, and understood in covenants, is still key to an understanding of love in the Hebrew Bible in general.

For example, take Moran's argument that *ahav* in covenants has political connotations. This holds even in stories that do not centrally concern these agreements. As I will show in subsequent chapters, love is intricately tied to power, especially political power, influencing who gets to be the subject of love and who gets to be its object, and whether a character loses or obtains power. This continued political resonance of love undoubtedly stems from its presence in covenants. Covenants, after all, as I explained, are based on and parallel other political agreements from the ancient Near East, especially suzerain-vassal treaties, which are agreements made between parties with differing amounts of power. Because of the use of *ahav* in political contracts, love therefore continues to be associated with things related to power, especially political power.

The theological resonance of *ahav*, which overlaps and intersects with its political meaning, can be explained similarly. For example, as I explain in the next chapter, the story about Rebekah's love of Jacob connects love both to theological concerns, such as divine preference, divine paternity, favoritism, and election, and also to political concerns, such as national identity and

---

45. Luc, "The Meaning of *'hb* in the Hebrew Bible," 47.

destiny. Similarly, the story of David and Saul, the subject of chapters 3 and 4, also associates love to both theological and political issues as it describes how God's favoritism or rejection leads to the gain and loss of love by others, which in turn leads to the gain and loss of political power. Considering that *ahav* is a key term used in covenants—that is, political agreements, which are centered on, arise from, and represent the special relationship between God and Israel—the theological and political resonances of love, which linger in stories throughout the biblical text, again appear to stem from the covenantal usage of this term.

The residual influence of love, moreover, also entails subjects Moran did not discuss in his short article, the most important of which are the kinship and familial resonances of *ahav*. As scholars have noted, the strange contrast between emotion and action stems from Moran's disregard of the centrality of kinship. That is, in the ancient Near East, and especially ancient Israel, society and everything in it, including politics and political agreements, were organized, envisioned, and described around ideas of the family.[46] For example, in these treaties, parties who were equal in power refer to each other as brothers, while in suzerain-vassal treaties, the vassal refers to himself as the son and the suzerain as his father. Unsurprisingly, this kinship language of father-son finds its way into Deuteronomy as well (Deut. 1:30–31; 8:5–6). Hence, considering the importance of kinship, ancient treaties and covenants were not simply impersonal agreements. Rather, they were more akin to adoptions or conversions.[47] They were a way to establish "fictive kinship bond," whereby "both parties agree to act like family"—that is, it was a way to "make kin out of nonkin."[48]

Considering the importance of family in the ancient Near East, Moran's understanding of *ahav* in the covenants as mainly entailing actions seems odder and more untenable. The concept of the family in no way aligns with an understanding of love as emotionless. For most of us, when we think about our family, we automatically feel something. Not always good things, of course, but something nonetheless. Though we may have unstated or stated obligations, promises, and agreements to and with our family members, and though they may influence how we act and behave, this certainly does not preclude emotion. Though unmentioned by Moran, Deuteronomy too, in its use of love, emphasizes the family as well as the emotions and actions associated with it. McCarthy, for example, though he agrees with Moran that love entails

---

46. Frank Moore Cross, "Kinship and Covenant in Ancient Israel," in *From Epic to Canon: History and Literature in Ancient Israel* (Baltimore: Johns Hopkins University Press, 1998), 3–21, esp. 11; Lapsley, "Feeling Our Way," 359; Levenson, *Love of God*, 22–26.

47. Levenson, *Love of God*, 23.

48. Richter, *Epic of Eden*, 57.

reverence and obedience to the terms of the covenant, points out that the father-son relationship, despite Moran's claims, is indeed present in Deuteronomy.[49] For example, Deuteronomy 14:1 explicitly calls Israelites the "children of the LORD your God," while Deuteronomy 8:5 likens God to a parent and Israel to the child that the parent disciplines.

This parent-child relationship, moreover, does not seem devoid of emotion. For example, Deuteronomy 1:30–31: "The LORD your God, who goes before you, is the one who will fight for you, just as he did for you in Egypt before your very eyes, and in the wilderness, where you saw how the LORD your God carried you, just as one carries a child, all the way that you traveled until you reached this place." Described in these verses are the actions taken by God for the welfare of Israel, which is likened to God's child. These deeds—protectively going in front in order to face the dangers head on and fighting for and even carrying the weary child until they reach a place of safety—express such care and tenderness that it is difficult to imagine them as lacking emotions and feeling. Indeed, though the word is not used here, these are actions indicative of love.

Another example, from Deuteronomy 7:7–8, though it does not explicitly mention the parent-child relationship, again emphasizes the importance of family to an understanding of love:

> It was not because you were more numerous than any other people that the LORD set his heart on you and chose you—for you were the fewest of all peoples. It was because the LORD loved you and kept the oath that he swore to your ancestors, that the LORD has brought you out with a mighty hand, and redeemed you from the house of slavery. . . .

According to these verses, God's actions—the deliverance of, selection of, and making covenants with Israel, covenants that center on the family—stem both from promises made to past family members ("ancestors") and also from love, a love that is gracious and unknowable, perhaps even irrational, and therefore likely also emotional.[50] These verses capture the heady mix of feeling, action, covenant, election, God, and family entailed in the understanding of love—an understanding that carries over into other stories about love that are not explicitly about the covenant, all of which, predictably, center on the family.

Finally, other features and aspects of love as evinced in covenants, which are unmentioned by Moran, also continue to have far-reaching influence on

49. McCarthy, "Notes on the Love of God," 144–47. See also McKay, "Man's Love for God," 426–35.

50. For more analysis on this verse, see Levenson, *Love of God*, 36–58.

stories in the Hebrew text. The most pervasive is the view of love as deadly, painful, and a source of suffering. In the following chapters, I show how love leads to negative ramifications, such as betrayal, violence, and even death. Tellingly, the negative ramifications of love often, though not always (e.g., the case of Jonathan), befall women characters, both those who love and those who are beloved.

These negative effects of love as well as its particular association with women again might stem from the use of love in covenants. Recall that covenants, where *ahav* is used and commanded, are binding agreements. That is, these agreements are enforceable and enforced. As the curses section of the covenant details, violations of the stipulations of the covenant (Deut. 27:11–26; 28:15–68), insofar as it shows a lack of love by the offender, have dire ramifications. In covenants, therefore, *ahav* is connected to and can cause both good things (i.e., blessings) and also bad things (i.e., curses). And this double-sided aspect of *ahav* in covenants, as well as the general understanding of love's power to cause both pleasure and pain, joy and suffering, might have led love to be associated with negative and ominous things in the Hebrew text.

Relatedly, the use of *ahav* in covenants might also explain why female characters in the biblical text, both those who love and those who are beloved, seem to fare especially badly in love. Recall that the covenant in Deuteronomy parallels suzerain-vassal treaties, that is, a treaty made between two parties with differing amounts of power, and that the higher power entity making the demands—the suzerain—is always a *male* emperor or king. As such, in the terms of covenant between God and Israel, Israel is always imagined as or likened to a person who is the less powerful family member. In Deuteronomy, as we saw, Israel is likened to a child or son: That is, someone whose age causes them to be hierarchically lower, while God is imagined or likened to a father or parent who is hierarchically higher (Deut. 1:30–31; 8:5–6; 14:1). Other books, such as Hosea and Ezekiel, use and reflect the same power configuration but with a slight twist. Israel is still imagined as the party with less power, but in these books, the power differential centers on gender. That is, in Hosea, Ezekiel, and other prophetic texts, Israel, identified by its principal city, Zion, or Jerusalem, is imagined as a female family member: namely, God's wife (Isa. 54:5–8; Jer. 2:23–3:10; Ezek. 16, 23; Hos. 2). Israel, however, is not a very good wife, but an uncontrollably lustful serial adulteress who constantly cheats on her husband: that is, God (Jer. 2:23–3:10; Ezek. 16, 23; Hos. 1–3). As if this were not disturbing enough, these metaphors—child and wife—are even conflated at times, as in Ezekiel 16 where Israel is disturbingly imagined as an abandoned orphan girl whom God raises and then marries.

The rich and disturbing portrayals of women in these texts have been well analyzed by scholars.[51] For our discussion, suffice it to say, the marriage metaphor both reflects and exacerbates the negative association between women and love—an association that again appears to be connected to the use and understanding of *ahav* in the covenant. Considering that marriages in the ancient world also entailed an agreement or covenant between parties with differing amounts of power, concerned family and kinship, and used the language of love, it is easy to see how the covenant between Israel and God can be reimagined and likened to a marriage covenant as it is in Hosea and Ezekiel. As such, just as Deuteronomy uses the father-son metaphor to foretell how Israel will repeatedly violate the covenant and incur harsh punishments as a result (Deut. 4:25–31; 30:1–3; 31:29), so Hosea and Ezekiel use a different family metaphor—the marriage metaphor—to describe the same thing: that is, the transgression of the covenant by Israel (Ezek. 16; Hos. 2).

Hosea, Ezekiel, and other prophetic texts therefore show the ease with which the violation of the covenant by Israel—a violation repeatedly warned about and foretold in Deuteronomy—can take on gendered meaning. That is, the violation of the covenant (or treaty) with its demand for love by the *male* sovereign, and the negative effects that originate from it, as Hosea and Ezekiel elucidate, can easily become associated with females. The patriarchal fear and suspicion of women, which was already present in the text, undoubtedly supported this negative association. As such, the negative effects that come from the failure to uphold the covenant and the lack of *ahav*, a term frequently used in these agreements to signify fidelity, can become particularly connected to women, especially in the Hebrew Bible, which was written, edited, and transmitted by men.

Finally, though unmentioned and unnoticed by scholars, love in the Hebrew text is also frequently associated with another interesting aspect: similarity. As I show in the following chapters, two characters who love each other are frequently depicted as similar to or mimicking each other. Though this similarity is a feature in modern love relationships as well (see chapter 2), this appears to be another aspect of love that arises from the use of *ahav* in covenants. Jaqueline Lapsley hints of this possibility in her discussion of Deuteronomy 10:18–19. In these verses, God, who is described as someone who loves strangers or foreigners (v. 18), commands the Israelites to love the stranger or foreigner as they "were strangers in the land of Egypt" (v. 19).

---

51. For a good example of feminist criticism of these passages as well as other narratives in the Hebrew Bible, see Gale A. Yee, *Poor Banished Children of Eve: Women as Evil in the Hebrew Bible* (Minneapolis: Fortress Press, 2003), esp. 81–134.

Though the mimicry in these verses is complex and multilayered, the association with love and similarity/likeness is evident. The reason why Israel is to love the foreigner "is to be in imitation of Yhwh's love for the stranger,"[52] that is, so Israel can act similarly to God. Moreover, in loving the stranger, not only are the Israelites mimicking God but also their former selves—when they were in dire need of God's help and, hence, God's love. The Israelites are to put themselves both in their own shoes and into those of God—and all of these shoe "replacements" are said to have something to do with love and similarity. Interestingly, this idea that love entails mimicry and likeness, which is evident in Deuteronomy in the description of the covenant, is found in narratives about love outside this book as well. Sometimes, as is the case of Deuteronomy 10:18–19, the direction and layers of the influence and mimicry are complex, and the meanings evinced are ambiguous. What is clear, however, is that the writers of the biblical text for some reason associate love and likeness.

CONCLUSION

This succinct overview of the history of scholarship on love shows that the complex meanings and associations of *ahav* comes from its prevalence and use in covenants, which in turn were influenced by ancient Near Eastern treaties. This overview of the centrality of covenants—the agreements of love—lays the groundwork for the chapters that follow where we turn to explore a selection of individual stories that feature or mention *ahav*. Because love in covenants, especially the one described in Deuteronomy, has theological, familial, social, political, and emotional valences, so also these valences bleed into the meaning of *ahav* in other narratives in the Hebrew text, even those that are not centrally about the covenant. Rather, like background music, these valences of covenantal love work in tandem with the unique features of an individual tale to elucidate and bring out specific features of love. As we will see in the subsequent chapters, the stories about love especially highlight the divinity of love, the power of love, the pain and mystery of love, and the gender of love. In evincing these matrices of meaning, which in turn help to expose particularities of love, covenants and the love found in them play a key role in the conception and understanding of love in the Hebrew Bible.

---

52. Lapsley, "Feeling Our Way," 363.

2

The Divinity of Love

Jacob and Esau

INTRODUCTION

If you have siblings, at some point you would have surely felt that you were
the victim of parental favoritism. This likely led to feelings of hurt and maybe
even dreams of besting the sibling so as to prove the utter foolishness of the
biased parent. Perhaps it is comforting to find this sense of familial injustice
in the Bible as well. Readers will have little trouble finding, if not solace, then
certainly resonance in the story of the twins Jacob and Esau. The tale, which
is the focus of this chapter, centers on the rivalry and competition of these
brothers, each of whom are loved and favored by one parent but not the
other. Because parental preference is intimately bound up with love, this story
conveys complex and intriguing ideas about love that help to further elucidate
how love, *ahav*, was imagined and understood in the biblical text.

As I will show in this chapter, though the story of Jacob and Esau conveys
the multivalent meanings and associations of covenantal love, it also focuses
and brings out a particular aspect of love: the divinity of love. This particular
aspect is elucidated by comparing love with its opposite—or more accurately,
something imagined as such. Though the true opposite of love is hate or perhaps the absence or lack of love, in the case of Jacob and Esau, love's opposite
is imagined as a different kind of love—a lower, inferior one. As I argue in
this chapter, the oppositional twins and oppositional love of the parents for
the twins are used to assert, compare, and assess two different kinds of loves:
a lofty, celestial love connected to God; and a baser, animal-like love centered
on appetites and bodily desires. Through this juxtaposition, the story asserts

29

the supremacy of the loftier kind of love by connecting it to God's preferences and plans. At the same time, however, the narrative undermines this loftier love by showing how it leads to betrayal, suffering, dysfunction, and the disintegration of the family. Through this wavering, the narrative wrestles with and posits the ultimate unknowability of love and the God behind it.

THE FAMILY HISTORY OF THE TWINS

The family history of Jacob and Esau reveals the pattern that drives their story and in so doing helps to elucidate their theological significance and provides insight into our understanding of love. To offer a brief summary of the narrative, Jacob and Esau are the twin sons of Rebekah and Isaac, and the grandsons of the Israelite matriarch and patriarch, Sarah and Abraham. Abraham, when he is still called Abram, receives a calling from God to leave his homeland and his former life behind (Gen. 12). For this bold undertaking, God makes a covenant with Abraham (called the Abrahamic covenant) promising him a particular parcel of land inhabited by the Canaanites as well as numerous descendants to settle this property, a formidable pledge considering that Abraham, at the time of his call, is seventy-five and childless (Gen. 12:4). This promise of numerous descendants and the land of Canaan (i.e., the promised land) to Abraham and his descendants by God is known as the Abrahamic promise, and it is the agreement upon which the divine election of Israel is centered. As recounted in Genesis, this promise and all that it entails will be passed on, like an inheritance, albeit a divine one, to particular descendant(s) of Abraham. After considerable family drama, Genesis 21:1–7 describes how God's promises to Abraham finally come to fruition with the miraculous birth of a son, Isaac, to his elderly and infertile wife, Sarah. It is Isaac who becomes the elect and inherits the Abrahamic promise from his father.

Isaac, however, does not accomplish this on his own. Rather, his mother, Sarah, clears or, more accurately, bulldozes the way for him. Sarah forces Abraham, with God's approval, to send away Isaac's competitor, his elder half-brother Ishmael along with Ishmael's mother, Hagar, Sarah's ex-slave (Gen. 21:8–20). As we are beginning to see, divine passivity and assent, parental favoritism, and ethically dubious actions undertaken by family members— especially mothers—to ensure the inheritance for their favored child represent long-standing traditions within this family. So too is the rivalry between siblings and the inevitable triumph by the younger child.

The above family background and its fractious dynamic set the scene for the birth of Isaac's rivalrous twin sons, Jacob and Esau, by Isaac's wife, Rebekah. In the ancient world, twin births, because they deviated from normal single births, were viewed as auspicious and extraordinary. More important, especially for the study of love, the birth of twins complicated the issue of inheritance as the two children were born nearly at the same time to the same mother. In the case of Jacob and Esau, it was not just money at stake with the inheritance but something far more priceless and theologically significant: elect status and a special relationship with God.

Considering this family history and the high stakes, the relationship between the brothers, unsurprisingly, is decidedly fraught from the outset. So fierce is their prenatal fighting that their mother, Rebekah, is even compelled to seek out God to figure out why the "children struggled together within her" (Gen. 25:22)—a rather benign translation of the Hebrew, which describes the twins as "dashing," "crushing," or "oppressing" each other in utero. During their private meeting, God, without either a mediator or Isaac present, tells the distraught Rebekah about the combative destiny of her forthcoming children:[1] "And the LORD said to her, 'Two nations are in your womb, and two peoples born of you shall be divided; the one shall be stronger than the other, the elder shall serve the younger'" (Gen. 25:23).

The translation of the last line of this oracle in the NRSV—"the elder shall serve the younger"—gives the false impression that the future of these twins is unambiguous and certain. The assuredness flattens the sense of volition and suspense that runs throughout this tale.[2] A better translation of the last line of the oracle (Gen. 25:23) would preserve its suspenseful ambiguity: it states both "the greater (or bigger) will serve the lesser (or smaller)," *and* "the lesser (or smaller) will serve the greater (or bigger)."[3] These translations better express the elusiveness of this oracle, which cryptically leaves the identity and the destiny of these twin siblings—that is, which brother is lesser or greater and who will serve whom—undetermined. Like all good oracles, it is phrased in such a way that it correctly foretells any and all futures, be it the triumph of Esau over Jacob or the reverse, that of Jacob over Esau. The truth is only discernible in hindsight.

What the oracle does clearly assert is that these twins will become the founders and representatives of rival nations; and, therefore, that the relationship between the brothers will have political and national implications that

1. Erin E. Fleming, "'She Went to Inquire of the Lord': Independent Divination in Genesis 25:22," *Union Seminary Quarterly Society* 60, no. 3 (2007): 1–10.

2. Elie Assis argues that Jacob is never permanently selected as the elect, but rather that there is a constant sense of expectation, a constant working toward election between the twins (*Identity in Conflict: The Struggle between Esau and Jacob, Edom and Israel*, Siphrut 19 [Winona Lake, IN: Eisenbrauns, 2016]).

3. For more on the story of Jacob and Esau's rivalry, see Carolyn Helsel and Song-Mi Suzie Park, *The Flawed Family of God: Stories of the Imperfect Families of Genesis* (Louisville: Westminster John Knox, 2021), esp. 115–17.

affect the understanding of love. The description of these twins immediately
after their birth brings out their political significance. Esau who comes out of
the womb first is described as red (*'admoni*) and hairy (*se'ar*) (Gen. 25:25). This
description puns with Edom, the red-soiled nation that claims Esau as their
forefather, of which Seir is a significant region (Gen. 32:3; 36:8–9; Num. 24:18;
Judg. 5:4; Ezek. 35:2–15). Jacob follows Esau, emerging from the womb literally on the heels of or, more accurately, grasping the heel of his older brother
(Gen. 25:26). As commentators have noted, the description of Jacob's unusual
means of entering the world offers a nifty wordplay between "heel" (*'aqev*)
and "Jacob" (*ya'aqov*) and also expresses the ingrained and therefore perpetual
competitive states of the brothers as well as the nations and people they will
beget and represent.[4]

The rivalry between the twins heats up when they grow up and are, unsurprisingly, shown to have different, indeed, contrasting personalities. Genesis
25:27 describes Esau as a "skillful hunter, a man of the field," that is, a rug-
ged outdoorsmen and hunter who, some have speculated, represents the very
embodiment of that which is uncouth, uncivilized, or feral.[5] In contrast,
Jacob is mysteriously described as a "quiet man, dwelling in tents." That is,
someone civilized, cultured, or possibly even feminine.[6]

Adding to the contrast and exacerbating the sibling rivalry, each of the
parents, Isaac and Rebekah, is said to love and favor one of the twins, but
seemingly not the other: "Isaac loved Esau, because he was fond of game;
but Rebekah loved Jacob" (Gen. 25:28). Considering the significance of these
characters as well as the use of *ahav*, Genesis 25:28 hints that something more
important is at stake than your run-of-the-mill parental preference. Moreover, the oppositional phrasing of the verse—Isaac loved Esau, but Rebecca
loved Jacob—hints that this love is oppositional and mutually exclusive for
some reason: Isaac's love for Esau precludes his love of Jacob, and Rebekah's
love of Jacob precludes her love for Esau. The contrasting and oppositional
love of the parents matches the contrasting and oppositional characterization of the twins. As we will see, the oppositional love of the parents not only

4. M. Malul, "*'āqēb* 'Heel' and *'āqab* 'To Supplant' and the Concept of Succession in the
Jacob-Esau Narratives," *Vetus Testamentum* 46, fasc. 2 (1996): 190–212.

5. Nahum Sarna, *Genesis=Be-reshit: the Traditional Hebrew Text with the New JPS Translation*
(Philadelphia: Jewish Publication Society, 1989), 181; E. A. Speiser, *Genesis* (Garden City:
Doubleday, 1964), 196.

6. Susan Niditch, *My Brother Esau Is a Hairy Man: Hair and Identity in Ancient Israel* (New York:
Oxford University Press, 2008), 115–17. See also Gregory Mobley, "The Wild Man in the
Bible and the Ancient Near East," *Journal of Biblical Literature* 116, no. 2 (1997): 217–33, and his
larger work, *Samson and the Liminal Hero in the Ancient Near East* (New York: T&T Clark, 2006),
esp. 43–45; Yael S. Feldman, "'And Rebecca Loved Jacob', But Freud Did Not," *Jewish Studies
Quarterly* 1, no. 1 (1993/94): 72–88.

will exacerbate the competition between the brothers, but, in so doing, will help to bring about the twins' contrasting destinies and reveal love's complex meanings.

REBEKAH'S LOVE OF JACOB

In contrast to Isaac, whose love of Esau is due to Isaac's love of game meat (Gen. 25:28), a fascinating rationale to which I will turn later in this chapter, the biblical text never gives a reason for Rebekah's love of Jacob. Though the motivations of characters, especially female characters, are frequently lacking in the Hebrew Bible, the absence of an explanation for Rebekah seems intentional when compared to the explanation, albeit odd, given for Isaac's love of Esau. The absence is even more striking considering that Rebekah is the first out of only three female characters in the Hebrew text who is said to love another person, thereby making her and her love unique.[7] (Her love as well as those of the other female characters are the subject of the last chapter.)

Clues in the biblical text suggest some possible motivations behind Rebekah's love of Jacob and why they might be unstated in the text. Considering that this story centers on the parents' oppositional love of their oppositional twins, opposites likely are key to this mystery. Indeed, the *lack* of mention of Rebekah's motivation stands in direct contrast to the *repeated* mention of Isaac's motivation, which is centered on food (Gen. 25:28; 27:4, 9, 14). As such, the reason why Rebekah loves Jacob likely contrasts with the reason for Isaac's love of Esau (provision of game meat). Moreover, if Isaac's reason is explicable and known, so much so that it is repeated, it follows that Rebekah's reason must be the opposite, that is, something ineffable, inexplicable, or unknown. Perhaps even Rebekah herself does not fully understand her mysterious love and preference for Jacob.

Moreover, this emphasis on opposites forces us to compare Isaac and Rebekah in order to figure out why they react so differently to their twins. And when we do so, we again encounter an opposite: Isaac's interaction with God with regard to his children stands in stark contrast to Rebekah's. While Isaac remains silent and on the sidelines after his short and immediately successful prayer for his infertile wife (Gen. 25:21), Rebekah is forced by her difficult pregnancy to seek divine consultation (Gen. 25:22). Though the matriarch's reaction initially might seem customary, Rebekah's private meeting with God to discuss her pregnancy is, first and foremost, otherwise unheard of in

7. The other two female subjects of love are Ruth (Ruth 4:15) and Michal (1 Sam. 18:20).

the Hebrew text.[8] Rather, though God talks directly to Abraham about his descendants (Gen. 15:4–5; 17), God is rather taciturn around female characters, always employing an intermediary, such as an angel (Hagar in Gen. 16:7–16 and Samson's mother in Judg. 13:3) or a cultic figure (Hannah in 1 Sam. 1). Even Sarah, the wife of Abraham, only learns about her future pregnancy indirectly when she eavesdrops on God and Abraham's conversation (Gen. 18:9–15).[9] Hence, Rebekah's private and direct tête-à-tête with God about her pregnancy is highly unusual and suggests a more intimate relationship between these two characters.

The unique interaction between Rebekah and God also speaks to the special nature of her children, the twins. To understand the significance of twins, a quick explication of their symbolism and cultural meanings is needed. As I previously noted, twins were considered special and auspicious because they deviated from normal single births.[10] As a result, they had ambivalent meanings. Twinship signaled heightened fertility—a positive attribute considering that Rebekah and Isaac's twins, or one of them at least, was supposed to carry on the Abrahamic promise and have innumerable descendants. However, the super fertility associated with twins also had a negative valence. Because twins entailed two children, they were sometimes suspected of being the result of adultery and the offspring of two different fathers.[11] Moreover, because usually animals, not humans, birthed multiple offspring from different fathers at one time (known as "heteropaternal superfecundation" or "double paternity"), twins were frequently associated with animals in myths and stories, especially disguise, transmutation, and transformation into them.[12] Indeed,

---

8. Noting the oddness of this direct divine consultation, interpreters posit that Rebekah went to a cultic site and utilized an intermediary. Gerhard von Rad, *Genesis*, trans. John H. Marks (Philadelphia: Westminster, 1961), 26; John A. Hartley, *Genesis* (Peabody: Hendrickson, 2000), 235–36; George W. Coats, *Genesis*, vol. 1 (Grand Rapids: Eerdmans, 1983), 184; J. P. Fokkelman, *Narrative Art in Genesis: Specimens of Stylistic and Structural Analysis* (Amsterdam: Assen, 1975), 88n4.

9. Fleming, "'She Went to Inquire of the Lord,'" 1–10; Victor P. Hamilton, *The Book of Genesis: Chapters 18–50* (Grand Rapids: Eerdmans, 1990), 177; Tikva Frymer-Kensky, *Reading the Women of the Bible: A New Interpretation of Their Stories* (New York: Schocken, 2002), 16.

10. Victor Turner states that the reality of twins therefore "presents the paradoxes that what is physical[ly] double is structurally single and what is mystically one is empirically two" (*The Ritual Process: Structure and Anti-Structure* [New York: Routledge, 1969], 45).

11. Veronique Dasen, "Becoming Human: From the Embryo to the Newborn Child," in *The Oxford Handbook of Childhood and Education in the Classical World*, ed. Judith Evans Grubbs and Tim Parkin (New York: Oxford University Press, 2013), 20; Gary Granzberg, "Twin Infanticide: A Cross-Cultural Test of a Materialistic Explanation," *Ethos* 1, no. 4 (1973): 405–12, esp. 406; Elizabeth Stewart, *Exploring Twins: Towards a Social Analysis of Twinship* (New York: St. Martin's Press, 2000), 20.

12. Turner, *Ritual Process*, 47.

Jacob, who is a twin, will go on to marry two sisters named Leah, "cow," and Rachel, "ewe" (Gen. 29:15–30).

Most important, as we have already seen with Jacob and Esau, twins often represented polarities and contradictions and as a result were viewed as having a "mediating function between animality and deity."[13] Twins, therefore, were associated with both animals and also the opposite: that is, the divine. They were "at once more than human and less than human."[14] This mediating, liminal aspect of twins led to starkly different reactions. Sometimes one or both of the twins were killed.[15] At other times, as shown by the stories of Herakles and Iphicles, Castor and Polydeuces, and Helen and Clytemnestra, and the gnostic narrative about Jesus and Thomas, the opposite occurred, and one or both of the twins were imbued with "special status, often with sacred attributes."[16] This special status centered on the twins' paternity. In these Greco-Roman myths, for example, twins did not just have two fathers, but two different "kinds" of them. One of the fathers of the twins was often imagined as a god or demigod who sometimes took on the guise of an animal. The other father, predictably, was a mere mortal. As a result of this oppositional divine-human paternity, one of the twins was viewed as "normal," human, and mundane while the other, in contrast, was imagined as sacred and semidivine, with a special destiny.

Some of these literary features found in other twin myths can also be detected in the story of the Israelite twins Jacob and Esau. The most important is the possible double paternity of Jacob and Esau, something which the text hints at but never confirms. One clue is the uniqueness of Rebekah's visit to God, which suggests a rather close relationship between the two. Indeed, while God is more involved than usual with Rebekah's pregnancy, Isaac, in contrast, is depicted as less involved than usual. After Isaac prays about his wife's infertility, Rebekah immediately conceives despite any mention of Isaac's "involvement" (Gen. 25:21). That is, unlike in most cases in the Hebrew Bible, the text never states that Isaac slept with, or "knew," his wife. Rebekah therefore swings rapidly from infertility to pregnancy with little to no participation by Isaac—at least none directly stated in the text.

The unusual prenatal actions and reactions by Rebekah, Isaac, and God, as well as the oppositional personalities of the twins, hint that the twins—or at least one of them—might be the result of an unusual amount of divine

13. Turner, *Ritual Process*, 47.
14. Turner, *Ritual Process*, 47.
15. Granzberg, "Twin Infanticide," 405–12.
16. Lloyd R. Bailey, "The Cult of the Twins at Edessa," *Journal of the American Oriental Society* 88, no. 2 (1968): 342–44; see also Leon D. Hankoff, "Why the Healing Gods are Twins," *The Yale Journal of Biology and Medicine* 50 (1977): 307–19, esp. 311; Turner, *Ritual Process*, 46.

involvement, perhaps even direct involvement.[17] Indeed, Jacob's possible divine paternity would make sense. Jacob, after all, not only has his name changed to Israel later in the narrative (Gen. 32:27–28) but also, as the oracle foretells, will come to beget, embody, and represent Israel—a nation that has a special status as God's elect and, therefore, is the bearer of a special, sacred destiny (Gen. 12:2–3).

Circling back to love, the putative double paternity also offers an explanation for the oppositional love of the parents: Rebekah might love Jacob because she both suspects and hopes that he is the twin with divine paternity and, therefore, the one with a special destiny. Though the reason for her love is missing, her actions provide evidence of her desires as well as how she ultimately chose to interpret God's ambiguous oracle. Considering that she is said to love only Jacob and, as we will see, goes out of her way to help him, it appears that she has interpreted the oracle in such a way that biases her toward a son whom she already prefers. That is, the motivations underlying Rebekah's love of Jacob might be intentionally absent in the text so as to show that she herself does not fully understand or comprehend her mysterious preference for Jacob. She loves Jacob without reason or rhyme but simply because she was meant to. Hence, Rebekah, who already loves and prefers Jacob for some unknown reason, through her actions tries to ensure that her interpretation of the oracle comes to pass. And in so doing, Rebekah becomes a participant in the fulfillment of this destiny—a destiny that has unforeseen and devastating consequences for Rebekah.

As such, Rebekah's love, which drives and helps fulfill Jacob's progression toward becoming Israel, at the end goes back to an unstated and mysterious source. No reason is given for why she initially favors this son and therefore chooses and wants him to be the special, chosen child. Hence, textual silence or absence in the description of Rebekah and her love of Jacob is perhaps the most apt rendering of this love and the unknowable reasons behind it. Perhaps Rebekah feels bad for Jacob as the second-born son or because Isaac so clearly favors Esau. Perhaps she resonates more with Jacob than with Esau because Jacob is portrayed as more similar to herself. Or maybe Rebekah recognizes or is influenced—lured even—by the possible semidivine nature of Jacob. Perhaps it is Jacob's status as the younger son that endears Jacob to Rebekah, as it is always the younger sons (c.f. Isaac, Jacob, Joseph, David, Solomon)—the underdog—whom God ends up mysteriously choosing and favoring in the

---

17. The other time there is a visit by a divine being followed by immediate conception by an infertile woman without the mention of the involvement of the husband is Samson. And scholars have wondered whether Samson, who is very similar to Herakles/Hercules is also imagined as half-divine. See Susan Niditch, *Judges: A Commentary* (Louisville: Westminster John Knox Press, 2008), 9, 168.

Hebrew Bible.[18] Her love seems to stem from a mixture of her own unstated assumptions and wishes as well as something like providence. Hence, both divinely ordained fate and human action and desire play a part in the fulfillment of Jacob's destiny to become Israel, the elect nation of God.

LOVE AND SIMILARITY

Isaac's love might be similarly motivated. That is, Isaac's love and preference for Esau might also arise from a mixture of fate, human motivations, and suspicions of double paternity. As Rebekah mysteriously loves Jacob because she suspects and wishes for him to be the divine twin, so also Isaac's preference and love for Esau might originate from his own inkling that Esau is the twin who is his true son. A notable feature of the parents' oppositional love suggests this is the case. Namely, each parent is depicted as preferring and loving the twin who is similar to themselves. As we will see in other chapters, similarity is shown to be an aspect of love in the Hebrew Bible, with characters often described as loving those whom they mirror and parallel.

The connection between similarity and love goes beyond the biblical text. Interestingly, though Rebekah, Isaac, Jacob, and Esau are fictional characters in ancient Hebrew folklore, modern psychology also notes the connection between love, especially romantic love, and likeness. As researchers have noted, people subconsciously and somewhat narcissistically gravitate toward those who look like or are similar to them, be they human or animal.[19] Funny posts about pet "mini-me's," "Boyfriend Twins," or articles such as "Science Says We All Just Want to Date Ourselves"[20] speak to this widespread tendency. Indeed, the social neurologist Stephanie Cacioppo notes that humans

18. Susan Niditch, *A Prelude to Biblical Folklore: Underdogs and Tricksters* (San Francisco: Harper & Row, 1987).

19. Jamie Ducharme, "Why Do So Many Couples Look Alike? Here's the Psychology behind the Weird Phenomenon," *Time*, April 4, 2019, https://time.com/5553817/couples-who-look-alike/; Berit Brogaard, "Are We Attracted to People Who Look Like Us?" *Psychology Today*, May 13, 2015, https://www.psychologytoday.com/us/blog/the-mysteries-love/201505/are-we-attracted-people-who-look-us; Gwendolyn Seidman, "Why Do We Like People Who Are Similar to Us?" *Psychology Today*, December 18, 2018, https://www.psychologytoday.com/us/blog/close-encounters/201812/why-do-we-people-who-are-similar-us; Amanda Chatel, "Science Says We All Just Want to Date Ourselves," *Bustle*, April 13, 2016, https://www.bustle.com/articles/153908-why-were-attracted-to-people-who-are-just-like-us-according-to-science.

20. David Robson, "Dogs Look Like Their Owners—It's a Scientific Fact," *BBC*, November 12, 2015, https://www.bbc.com/future/article/20151111-why-do-dogs-look-like-their-owners.
Romantic doppelgangers on Twitter: @alunesz, "10/10 can relate. Definitely my soulmate and definitely not related," Twitter, July 6, 2018, https://twitter.com/alunesz/status/1015121877424136193?ref_src=twsrc%5Etfw%7Ctwcamp%5Etweetembed%7Ctwterm%5E1015121877424136193&ref_url=https%3A%2F%2Fwww.huffpost.com%2Fentry%2Fwhy

possess mirror neurons that encourage a kind of reciprocal mirroring among lovers. That is, we naturally love and are loved by those whom we resemble; and in our love, we come to mirror our beloveds and our beloveds come to mirror us.[21]

Two episodes that follow the initial descriptions of the twins reveal Rebekah and Isaac's tendency to love the child whom they resemble. Genesis 25:29–34 describes how Esau, coming in from the field, encounters Jacob cooking a lentil stew and, famished, requests some of it. Jacob, in turn, responds that he will surely share his food with his brother—albeit, for an exorbitant price: Esau's firstborn birthright, which is essentially double the portion of the inheritance. To this obvious price gouging, Esau readily agrees, trading away his firstborn inheritance for a pittance.

Neither twin comes off well in this episode. Jacob is portrayed as clever and ambitious but also unethical and unbrotherly, having no qualms about taking advantage of family members, especially at their point of weakness. Esau, in contrast, seems softheaded and shortsighted. Unlike Jacob, who understands the long-term value of the inheritance, Esau cannot think beyond the immediate gratification of his growling stomach: "Esau said, 'I am about to die; of what use is a birthright to me?'" (Gen. 25:32). Animal-like in his hunger, Esau is also depicted as barely able to speak, using a word for the feeding of animals (*la'at*) to demand some of Jacob's stew, which he boorishly calls "this red, red stuff" (Gen. 25:30).[22] In contrast to the animal-like, animal-hunting Esau, Jacob is portrayed as the very opposite: domestic and civilized, quietly engaged in an activity associated with society and culture—cooking.[23] As such, Jacob undoubtedly is paralleled and aligned with his mother, Rebekah, who, as a female, is connected to domestication, socialization, and culture in the ancient Near East and the Hebrew Bible (Gen. 2:4–3:24; Judg. 16).

Another episode further confirms and highlights the parallels between Jacob and Rebekah. Genesis 27 describes how Jacob, with the help of his mother, dupes his now blind father, Isaac, into giving him the blessing meant for Esau. As a prelude to the reception of the blessing, Esau is sent out to hunt so as to prepare a last meal for his father. In Esau's absence, Jacob, following

---

-we-date-lookalike_n_5bbf96f4e4b0bd9ed55818. See also Tumblr of "boyfriendtwin": https://boyfriendtwin.tumblr.com/. Chatel, "Science Says We All Just Want to Date Ourselves," n.p.

21. Stephanie Cacioppo, *Wired for Love: A Neuroscientist's Journey Through Romance, Loss, and the Essence of Human Connection* (New York: Flatiron Books), esp. 74–80.

22. Robert Alter, "Sacred History and the Beginnings of Prose Fiction," *Poetics Today* 1, no. 3 (1980): 159; Yair Zakovitch, *Jacob: Unexpected Patriarch*, trans. Valerie Zakovitch (New Haven: Yale University Press, 2012), 23.

23. Claude Levi-Strauss, *Introduction to a Science of Mythology*, vol. 1, *The Raw and the Cooked*, trans. John and Doreen Weightman (New York: Harper & Row, 1969); Richard W. Wrangham, *Catching Fire: How Cooking Made Us Human* (New York: Basic Books, 2009).

the instructions of his mother, disguises himself as his hairy and animal-like older brother by donning the skin and fur of a goat and receives the blessing in Esau's place. This episode reveals the shared qualities of mother and son. Active, ambitious, deceptive, and even unethical, mother and child appear to have little qualms about working in tandem to lie to and exploit their more dupable family, especially when they are debilitated or at a point of weakness. No wonder Rebekah prefers and loves Jacob and acts as if he is the divine twin with the divine destiny. His ambition and trickster nature matches her own.

Moreover, the larger structure of their stories confirms that Rebekah and her beloved Jacob are parallel—or twins, as it were. Rebekah moves from Aram to Canaan to marry Isaac in Genesis 24, while Jacob, her double, later inverses and retraces her journey as he flees Canaan only to end up in his mother's hometown in Aram (Gen. 29). There he, like his mother, finds a spouse—two spouses, in fact, in the form of his cousins Rachel and Leah, sisters who are also depicted as oppositional twins.[24] Indeed, following the tendency of doubles to duplicate exponentially, Jacob's rivalry with Esau will be mimicked and replayed in the rivalry between Jacob's sister-wives. Like Esau and Jacob, so Leah, the elder, fertile, and unloved wife of Jacob, will struggle with her younger sibling, Rachel, who, in contrast, is beautiful, infertile, and beloved by Jacob (Gen. 29:1–30:24). Considering that Rachel is depicted as very similar to Jacob, similarity again is shown to be an important aspect of love. And just as the similarity between Jacob and Rachel plays a role in his love of Rachel, so the similarity between Rebekah and Jacob likely plays a role in Rebekah's love of Jacob.

ISAAC'S LOVE OF ESAU (AND FOOD)

Similarity also explains Isaac's love of Esau. Like Rebekah with Jacob, Isaac seems equally motivated to love Esau because of parallels between himself and the older twin—parallels which might also indicate that Esau, not Jacob, is probably his true son. Unlike with Rebekah, however, the biblical text offers a reason, albeit cryptic, for Isaac's love of Esau: "Isaac loved Esau, because he was fond of game" (Gen. 25:28). Though this explanation initially seems trivial, Isaac's love of tasty meat dishes appears to be a defining characteristic of this figure, mentioned several times in the biblical text (Gen. 25:28; 27:4, 9, 14).[25] As such, it seems to convey something more than that Isaac was an

---

24. Samuel Dresner, "Rachel and Leah: Sibling Tragedy or the Triumph of Piety and Compassion?," *Biblical Review* 6, no. 2 (1990): 22–27, 20–42.

25. Jens A. Kreuter, "Warum liebte Isaak Esau?" *Biblische Notizen* 48 (1989): 17–18.

ancient foodie. Rather, considering that the most frequent occurrence of *ahav* in the story of Jacob and Esau concerns Isaac's love of food, it seems to be key to an understanding of Isaac and his love, especially his love of Esau.

Tellingly, three out of the other four statements about Isaac's love (*ahav*) of food occurs in the story of the theft of Esau's blessing (Gen. 27:4, 9, 14). As I noted, Genesis 27 describes the blind Isaac instructing Esau to go and hunt game so that this twin can prepare him a tasty meat dish, which Isaac loves (*ahav*) (v. 4) before receiving the blessing.[26] (Blessings in the Hebrew text were not simply nice statements but incontrovertible magical word-acts and, as such, were serious business.) While Esau is out hunting, Rebekah overhears the conversation between Isaac and Esau, repeats it to Jacob, again mentioning Isaac's love (*ahav*) of meat dishes (v. 9). She then instructs Jacob to get some animals from their flock so that she can cook a tasty meat meal from it, as Isaac loves (*ahav*) (v. 9), so that Jacob can pretend to be Esau and be blessed in place of his twin. Despite the unlikelihood of success[27]—at one point in the story Isaac wonders aloud why the voice of the son before him is Jacob's and not Esau's (Gen. 27:22)—Jacob and Rebekah succeed in their ruse, and Jacob obtains the blessing meant for Esau.

Considering that Genesis 27 mentions Isaac's love (*ahav*) of meaty dishes three times, it appears that Isaac's gastronomic proclivities play a central role in the success of Rebekah and Jacob's trick. The blind Isaac appears to have been hoodwinked and further blinded because of his love of tasty meat dishes—so blinded in fact that he is tricked out of giving the blessing to the meat-providing son he prefers and loves. No wonder the author of Proverbs, using the same word for a delicious dish as is used of Isaac's desired food in Genesis 27 (*mat'am*), warns: "Do not desire the ruler's delicacies [*mat'am*] for they are deceptive food" (Prov. 23:3). Bespeaking their similarity, food seems to be a weakness and a source of blindness for both Esau and Isaac. Just as Esau is blinded by his brother's cuisine to trade his birthright for some worthless stew (Gen. 25:29–34), so also is the blind Isaac swindled by Jacob with a beloved meaty meal.

The use of food in both manipulations, especially food made from animal flesh in the case of Isaac, parallels Esau and Isaac and, in so doing, conveys criticism of them. Both Esau and Isaac are taken advantage of because they

---

26. The word used in this verse to describe the food dishes is *ahav*. However, the NRSV translation seems uncomfortable with the use of love here and instead renders it as "like": "Then prepare for me savory food, such as I *like*, and bring it to me to eat, so that I may bless you before I die" (emphasis added).

27. Later sources, such as Jubilees 26:17–18, even argue that God deliberately "blinded" Isaac so that Jacob would receive the blessing. For other sources, see: James Kugel, *The Bible as It Was* (Cambridge: Belknap Press of Harvard University Press, 1997), 210.

allow their appetite for food—that is, their stomach and their bodily and animal comfort and desires—to override their intellect, rationality, and wisdom. Hence, in contrast to the clever and cultured Rebekah and Jacob, Isaac and Esau are portrayed as somewhat uncultured and uncouth—as ruled by their baser, animal-like appetites.

Indeed, it is telling that the few stories we have about Isaac center on him almost being sacrificed by his own father (Gen. 22); relieving himself in a field when he first meets his future wife (Gen. 24:62–65);[28] being discovered fondling, that is "playing" with (or as the Hebrew puts it, using his name as a verb, "Isaac-ing") his wife (Gen. 26:8); and finally, being duped by his wife and son while waiting for a meal (Gen. 27). The tales about Isaac's near sacrifice, his embarrassing meet-cute, his secret fondling, and hoodwinking all center on the body and what comes in and out it. They entail bodily appetites, be it the need for sex, food, or excretion.

Even the most famous episode associated with Isaac—his near sacrifice by his father, Abraham (Gen. 22)—concerns consumption, especially of animals, as sacrificed animals would be consumed by people and also by the gods or God in the form of smoke. This story, which explores the difference between humans and animals, especially as sacrifice, centers on the substitution of a human being, Isaac, for the animal sacrifice.[29] Genesis 22 therefore likens Isaac, whose portrayal emphasizes his animal-like and bodily appetites, to an animal, one which is nearly sacrificed as a whole burnt offering. However, at the end, the story also affirms the difference between humans and animals as it describes Isaac's last minute salvation by a divinely appointed appearance of a ram to serve as his substitute (Gen. 22:13).

Hence, the close association of this patriarch with animals parallels him to the son he loves who is also portrayed as similar to an animal, and explains Isaac's attraction to and preference for Esau. As I noted earlier, Esau is described as a feral, outdoorsy hunter who runs around in fields—that is, he behaves like a predatory, carnivorous beast. Additionally, in Genesis 27:27, Isaac, despite noticing that the voice belongs to Jacob, is convinced that the son in front of him is truly Esau once he feels and smells Jacob. Jacob, as I stated earlier, has disguised himself as the hairy Esau by putting on the skin and fur of a baby goat. Considering that Isaac, when Jacob draws near, exclaims that his son feels and smells like Esau, Esau must smell and feel like a goat! Isaac's delight at the goat-like smell and feel of Esau indicates that it is the animal-like aspect of Esau that endears him to Isaac. That is, Isaac's love

28. Joel Kaminsky, "Humor and the Theology of Hope: Isaac as a Humorous Figure," *Interpretation* 54 (2000): 363–75, esp. 369.

29. Jon D. Levenson, *The Death and Resurrection of the Beloved Son: The Transformation of Child Sacrifice in Judaism and Christianity* (New Haven: Yale University Press, 1993).

of Esau seems to be intimately connected to, even extend from, his connection to animals and his love of them, especially his appetite for dishes created from their flesh. Hence, it makes sense that Isaac would prefer and love Esau, and not Jacob. Esau provides and also smells and feels like the animals that the animal-like (Gen. 22) Isaac loves to eat.

THE OPPOSITIONAL LOVES OF ISAAC AND REBEKAH

This heavy emphasis on animals in the story of Jacob and Esau is perhaps unsurprising. As I noted earlier, twins were likened to animals, especially transformation into them, because they, like animals, were evidence of superfecundation or double paternity. The narrative intentionally stresses this connection between animals and twins by having Jacob dress up as the hairy, goat-like Esau who is beloved by the animal-like and animal-loving Isaac. By depicting human characters and animals as possible substitutions for each other and as taking on the other's disguise, the narrative likens humans and animals and intentionally plays up and blurs the distinction between them. This has implications for our understanding of love. As a result of this alignment between humans and animals, Isaac's appetitive, bodily based love of things that resemble animals or are made from animals is depicted as a hybrid—as both animalistic and also human. Therefore, the love that Isaac has for Esau is portrayed as one that leans into or reflects the animal part of human beings.

Most important, the animal-like aspects of human characters from which this appetitive, base love arises are placed in contrast with nonanimal, nonappetitive, and nonhuman love: a love that comes from a higher source, from something that does not suffer from weaknesses or deficiencies of the body— that is, from God or the gods, and as such is divine or sacred (Isa. 40:28). Tellingly, in the Hebrew Bible, the separation between the divine and the human/animal centers around food and eating. For example, several stories in the Hebrew text describe how divine beings or angels refuse to eat food provided by their human hosts. These stories confirm that human foods and the hunger for them are categorically different from those of the gods (Judg. 6:19–21; 13:16). Food and the physical consumption of it therefore appears to entail a boundary that separates the gods from humans. Hence, the repeated mention of Isaac's love of meat dishes composed of flesh, albeit cooked flesh, in so far as they are in opposition to the smoke of sacrifices "consumed" by god/s, emphasizes and contrasts Isaac and, most importantly, his love with that of and from God/the gods.

This contrast between higher, divine love with lower, animalistic, appetitive love reveals the difference between—indeed, the contrasting nature of—Isaac's love and Rebekah's love. As I noted earlier, Rebekah loves Jacob for an unstated reason, perhaps because she hopes or suspects that he might be the divine twin with the divine destiny. In so doing, Rebekah, in her love of Jacob, unwittingly becomes a participant in the unfolding of a divine plan that leads to the election of Jacob, later renamed Israel. Her reason, though never forthrightly stated, nicely contrasts with Isaac's love of Esau, which, as I noted, is driven by his bodily desires, his appetite, something that is very human and animalistic—and something, therefore, that is the opposite of the divine. Indeed, what can be more contrastive of the mysterious and unrenderable sacred love that Rebekah has of Jacob than Isaac's animalistic, appetitive love for Esau, the oppositional twin of Jacob? The parents' oppositional "kind" of love of the oppositional twins therefore proceeds from oppositional reasons.

The contrasting love of the parents, moreover, might also reflect specula-tions about the double paternity of the twins. As I noted earlier, twins were frequently believed to be the children of two different fathers, one of whom was imagined as divine and the other imagined as human. As such, it might be that Rebekah's love and aid of Jacob come from her suspicions that Jacob is the divine twin; and similarly, Isaac's love for Esau might originate from a similar hunch. It is telling that Isaac's love of Esau, in so far as it is connected to his love of animals, is portrayed as appetitive, food-based, and ultimately, as I have argued, human. Perhaps it seems more likely to the animal-like, appetitive Isaac that Esau—the uncouth and outdoorsy son associated with hunting and the procurement of animals, the meat of which is consumed by animals and humans and indeed beloved by Isaac—is the twin who is actu-ally his child. Fearful of paternal fraud, the dupable, animal-like, meat-loving Isaac cannot but love and prefer Esau over against the tricky, tent-dwelling, lentil-cooking Jacob.

GOD'S LOVE AND PREFERENCE

Though it is clear that Isaac loves Esau and that Rebekah loves Jacob, where does God stand on the matter? Which twin does God love and favor? On one level, as these twins represent different nations and people, one of which is Israel, the final answer is clear. However, the story cleverly pushes the reader, despite their knowledge of the conclusion, to seek out the clues that speak to Jacob as the divinely chosen and divinely beloved. We have already seen one of these clues: God's unusually active participation with Rebekah's pregnancy, which subtly suggests the divine paternity of Jacob. Another clue concerns the opposite: God's silence. That is, while Jacob and Rebekah trick and deceive their more gullible family members out of the blessing and inheritance, God, one of the key characters of this drama, mysteriously remains on the sidelines. Why does God let these characters get away with their bad behavior, even allowing them to hoodwink Isaac, a patriarch of Israel?

Just as the absence of an explanation for Rebekah's love of Jacob is suggestive, so God's silence also speaks volumes. Though the text never gives a reason behind God's decision to stay out of the family squabble, God's inaction can be interpreted as tacit approval of the twin that God does love and favor. That is, perhaps God does not step in—never stops Jacob from offering Esau an unfair trade and never tells Isaac that he is being tricked—precisely because God wants Jacob to succeed and become the elect. One later source even goes so far as to suggest that God deliberately blinded Isaac so as to ensure the success of his chosen twin (Jub. 26:17–18).

If so, perhaps Rebekah's love and success are as unintended on her part as they are preordained. She is successful in her love and aid of Jacob because she is fated to love the same twin that God loves for some mysterious, unstated reason. (The implications of Rebekah's alignment with God's selection of Jacob are discussed in the last chapter.) Perhaps God loves and favors Jacob because Jacob has revealed himself to be more desirous or more capable of elect status and, therefore, more likely to succeed. Or, as I propose, perhaps God chooses Jacob because he is in fact the divine twin. The text leaves these motivations and reasons tantalizingly ambiguous. And as with Rebekah, the true source and reason for God's love and selection of Jacob/Israel remain shrouded in mystery. What is clear, however, is that it is Jacob—and the namesake nation that he begets and represents, Israel—whom God loves and chooses as the next bearer of the Abrahamic promise.[30] God's preferences and selection, though opaque in origin, therefore act as an invisible marker of the divinely chosen who in return receives love—the right kind of love—from others. This feature of love, that it is a cipher or marker of divine preference, will become increasingly conspicuous in the stories that I discuss in the next two chapters.

Hence, to summarize the argument thus far, by comparing and contrasting the twins as well as the love they receive, and by aligning one of the loves with God's plans and preferences, the two loves of the parents can be distinguished and evaluated. One love, that of Rebekah, is intertwined with divine election, and therefore shown to be superlative and divine. The other, in contrast, is aligned with animals, appetites, and the body and therefore shown to embody

---

30. Later, when the relationship between Israel and Edom has soured, the biblical writers will take advantage of the opposing characteristics of the twins to underscore and incontrovertibly assert the divine choice and love of Israel/Jacob over against Edom/Esau. Missing all the ambivalence and ambiguity of Genesis, Malachi 1:2–3 has God forthrightly declare, "Yet I have loved Jacob, but I have hated Esau." Compounding the interpretative problems, this theological challenging statement is repeated in Romans 9:13.

that which is the opposite of the divine. Therefore, as the first kind of love is said to reflect divine preference or selection, so the second love is said to reflect the opposite, a lack of selection by God—and therefore designated as the baser love. Hence, through the comparison and contrast of the oppositional "kinds" of love as embodied by the parents and their oppositional children, the narrative asserts and emphasizes how real love—the higher, better love—is a celestial one originating from, that is, "fathered" by, God.

THE DIVINITY OF LOVE

While the story of Jacob and Esau through a juxtaposition of different "kinds" of love brings out a particular feature of love, this does not mean that the polyvalent meanings evinced by covenantal love are absent. Rather, God's choice of Jacob/Israel, which overlaps with and perhaps even induces Rebekah's love, speak to the far-reaching influence of covenantal love. As we saw in the previous chapter, because of the use of *ahav* in covenants, love has theological, familial, political, social, and emotional valences that extend beyond these books. The story of Jacob and Esau reflects these different meanings of *ahav*. The theological and political overtones of love in this story are the easiest to recognize. As I explained, the juxtaposition of the oppositional love of the parents reflects two different kinds of loves—a baser, appetitive love and a superior, divine love—and is used to assert God's love and selection of Jacob/ Israel. Considering that Jacob is the eponymous ancestor of Israel, it is therefore evident that love conveys political and theological meanings.[31]

The political and theological valences bring out the societal significance of *ahav*: love is used in the story of Jacob and Esau to convey how Israel imagines and understands itself. To offer only a brief comment on a very complicated topic, the contrasting portrayals and the contrasting loves help to articulate and affirm Israelite identity, one which, like so many others, is created and

31. Especially interesting is the political valence of *ahav* which may help to explain the strangely exclusive and opposing love of the parents. Because these twins are not just individual characters but ciphers for different peoples, the parents' oppositional love for them is closely tied to and reflective of the political entities that they will become. As a result, though parents can and do love more than one of their children at the same time, this is not so in this case because these children represent different nations. Love, *ahav*, as I explained in the previous chapter, because of its use in suzerain-vassal treaties, entails meanings of covenantal love, that is, covenantal loyalty and obedience *to a particular suzerain*. And as one would not have pledged loyalty and love to multiple suzerains, so love is understood as something mutually exclusive, especially when applied to political entities. Therefore, as it would be a violation of the agreement to love two different suzerains, so Rebekah and Isaac can love either Jacob, that is, Israel, *or* Esau, that is, Edom, but not both. The love of these parents, Rebekah and Isaac, for these twins, Jacob and Esau—twins who represent different nations—must be mutually exclusive.

maintained through opposition or contrast to others, especially those that are similar to the self. Twins, because they are nearly the same yet different and distinct, are the perfect metaphor with which to engage over struggles of identity. This is the reason why twins, especially combative or oppositional twins, are so prevalent in foundational myths, which describe the origins, the coming into being, of particular cities, nations, or groups.[32]

Just as in these other foundation myths, the twinship of Jacob and Esau as well as the oppositional love of the parents is employed in a similar manner to outline and highlight the contours of Israelite identity: to define and articulate what Israel is by comparing it to what it is not. Jacob/Israel is Israel in so far as he/it is *not* Esau/Edom. Jacob/Israel is tricky, sophisticated, cultured, ambitious, and loved with a love that is high, divine, and sacred. Elected or chosen by God, he/it has a divine destiny. In contrast, Esau/Edom is *not* Jacob/Israel, in that he/it is uncouth, animalistic, stupid, gullible, and loved with a baser love that comes from animalistic and bodily needs, appetites, and desires. By showing the key difference between the twins, by showing what Jacob/Israel is not, Esau/Edom helps to stress and annunciate what Jacob/Israel is. Hence, the social valence of love works in conjunction with the theological and political meanings to bring out, formulate, and uphold Israel's identity.

The theological, political, and social aspects of love are undoubtedly central to the meanings reflected in this tale. However, if this story were only about these things, it would not be so memorable, impactful, or relatable. It would, in short, fail to express the full sense and significance of love. Rather, what gives this story poignancy and weight, and in so doing, reveals and reflects the fuller sense of love, are the emotions—the affective reactions and impact of love on various members of this family as shown by their actions and expressions. Hence, though largely disregarded by Moran in his work on covenantal love, at least in this biblical narrative and I suspect in others as well, the familial and emotional aspects of love are central to an elucidation of love's meaning and significance.

The most dramatic and telling emotions are expressed by the central victim of love in this story: Esau. Two instances in particular highlight his psychological anguish. Shortly after Jacob steals the blessing from his father, Esau returns to Isaac with a pre-blessing meal of wild game (Gen. 27:30–31). Discovering his brother's betrayal, Esau begs that things be made right: "Esau said to his father, 'Have you only one blessing, father? Bless me, me also, father!' And Esau lifted up his voice and wept" (Gen. 27:38). Esau's sad plea emphasizes the two-ness and twinship of himself and Jacob, as Esau *twice* begs his father

---

32. The most famous is the Roman twins: Romulus who kills his twin Remus during the founding of Rome.

to provide another blessing (Gen. 27:34, 38). Esau also notes how Jacob has taken advantage of him twice, first with the birthright (v. 36) and now with the blessing (v. 38). To a careful reader, the emphasis on doubles is disturbing and heartbreaking as it accentuates how Esau is betrayed not by just any *one*, but by *two* members of his family—his mother and brother. Adding insult to injury and further bringing out the significance of two, the culprit is his twin brother, someone who should have been his double and his closest ally but who instead has turned out to be the very opposite: his rival and enemy. The identity of the perpetrator—his twin brother—magnifies the emotional weight of the betrayal. No one can break your heart like family.

A second instance further illustrates Esau's pain. Shortly before Jacob's flight from the angry Esau and his departure to his mother's homeland, Jacob is warned by his father "not to marry one of the Canaanite women" (Gen. 28:6). Esau, realizing that his marriages to Canaanite women disappoint his father, futilely tries to copy Jacob by marrying women who are descended from Ishmael (Gen. 28:8–9). Esau, likely envious of things that Jacob has received as the recipient of the "right" kind of love, tries to act more like the beloved Jacob. Esau's imitation, predictably, is a failure. Ishmael, the ancestor of the women he marries, is not only Isaac's stepbrother, but, like Esau, is a firstborn son who was rejected as the inheritor of the Abrahamic promise. Esau, the rejected, in trying to mimic the beloved and chosen, ends up simply married into the family of another rejected kin, thereby compounding the rejected status. The unloved—or in the case of Esau, the one unloved by the right characters—can't catch a break, even when they try to act like the beloved.

Esau's emotional reactions and the feelings they evince of envy, disappointment, sadness, distress, and finally homicidal rage, reveal the emotional toll on those on the losing end of love. Perhaps a small amount of consolation can be found in the fact that it is not just the victim but the "criminal" of love—well, at least one of them—who suffers as a result of their actions. Shortly after his theft of the blessing, Jacob, in order to escape Esau's homicidal rage, takes his mother's advice to temporarily relocate to her hometown in Paddan-Aram. And while the twins do eventually reconcile, albeit ambivalently (Gen. 33), even coming together one last time to bury their father (Gen. 35:29), there is no mention of a reunion between Rebekah and her beloved son Jacob. Once Jacob leaves home for Paddan-Aram, Rebekah never sees Jacob again. This eternal separation, some argue, is both payback for Rebekah's participation in the deception and also an act of self-sacrifice. Rebekah tells a frightened Jacob that if their ruse during the blessing is discovered, she would take on any curse he might receive (Gen. 27:13). Though the ruse succeeds without a discovery or curse, Rebekah still seems to be punished for her actions—actions which stem from her love of Jacob.

Indeed, when it comes to love, the text seems a bit masochistic. Echoing Vincent van Gogh, the story seems to imply that "[t]he more you love, the more you suffer." It is, therefore, telling that in contrast to Rebekah, the other parent, Isaac, is never depicted as acting on behalf of his preferred, beloved son Esau. Rather, Isaac's inaction contrasts with Rebekah's involvement, hinting that her love is truer or deeper than that of Isaac's for Esau. Though both parents are said to love, their love clearly is not the same. Rather, as I outlined, Rebekah's love is the better love, the one that aligns with God's love and preferences. Yet in terms of suffering, Isaac's milquetoast love leads perhaps to a better conclusion: he passes on his inheritance, dies a peaceful death, and is buried by both sons. In contrast, Rebekah's more ardent love seems to generate more ardent suffering: eternal separation from her beloved.

It seems that love in the Hebrew Bible has a steep price. A small rundown of love's requirements as reflected in this story details its cost: For Esau, love entails suffering and betrayal. For Rebekah, it entails self-sacrifice, self-suffering in the place of the beloved, up to and including death or a curse, and also separation from the beloved. For this particular family, love demands all. As much as love can create a sense of unity and kinship, in this story of the twins, it causes conflict and dissolution. More distressingly, love can lead to love's opposite, hate—or at least something that looks and feels and expresses something uncomfortably similar to hate. It is, after all, Rebekah's love of Jacob that leads her to betray the love and trust of Isaac and Esau. Her love, in short, causes her and her beloved Jacob to treat other members of their family like an enemy.

Disturbingly, this all counts as success in this narrative. Rebekah's favoritism of Jacob is reflected in God's preference toward Jacob and his lineage. The familial destruction she causes and the grim problems associated with her love are more or less sanctioned by the outcome in the text. It seems we are to question whether hers is the right kind of love—whether it is indeed superior and divine in nature. This subversion is further evident in the sympathetic portrayal of Esau and Isaac, and conversely, the rather unsympathetic portrayals of Rebekah and Jacob. Mother and son are painted as coldhearted, callously taking advantage of unlucky family members who are left hurt, distraught, and angry.

Through these portrayals, the narrative compels the reader to ask troubling questions: If the love that Jacob receives from his mother aligns with and indeed consists of a better divine love, then why does it lead to such negative ramifications, such as pain, betrayal, suffering, and family fracturing? Should a love that is divinely approved lead to such unchecked unethical actions? Should it tear families apart? Is this really what love is? And if so, is love really connected to God and the divine? As the progression of the questions demonstrates, questions about love cannot but turn into questions about God. This is especially so in this case, as this story asserts one kind of love—the love that is intertwined and aligned with God and God's preferences and plans—over against another as the better, more authentic love. Hence, the sympathetic and pitiful portrayals of Esau and Isaac, as well as the contrasting unsympathetic and unethical portrayals of Jacob and Rebekah, compel the reader to question and struggle with the higher love represented and expressed by Rebekah; and also therefore with the God who is aligned with this love and who silently and passively allows such unethical acts to be done in love's name.

CONCLUSION

This chapter examined the story of the foundational twins, Jacob and Esau, each of whom is loved and favored by one parent but not the other. This exploration began with noticing the presence of opposites and contrasts, namely, the contrasting characterization of Jacob and Esau that paralleled the oppositional love of the parents, Rebekah and Isaac. A variety of reasons, such as suspicions of double paternity, likeness and similarity, God's mysterious preferences and plans, and, in the case of Isaac, appetitive tendencies, were posited as the reason behind the oppositional love of the parents.

More importantly, this chapter revealed that the contrasts, especially the oppositional love of Rebekah and Isaac, conveyed and emphasized a particular aspect of love: that "real" love is divine or, at the very least, very closely connected to God. By comparing the oppositional twins as well as the oppositional loves, two different kinds of loves were found to be present and compared. One kind of love—the love of Isaac for Esau—was shown to be a baser, animal-like love centered on appetites and bodily wants and needs. In contrast, the other—the love of Rebekah for Jacob—was depicted as closely aligned with God's preferences, plans, and ultimately selection. As such, this love as expressed by Rebekah was deemed superior to that of Isaac. Through distinguishing and weighing the two "kinds" of loves, the narrative asserts that the right kind of love finds its source in God with whom it is closely connected. However, by showing how this love—the one attributed to Rebekah and supported by God—leads to unethical actions, emotional distress, and familial discord and disintegration, the story expresses complicated feelings and struggles about love and also, by extension, about God, from whom this "true" love emanates.

3

The Power of Love

Saul and David

INTRODUCTION

The next two chapters explore one of the most celebrated heroes of the
Hebrew Bible, David, and the ways in which love is understood and reflected
in the stories about this beloved king. The general contours of David's story
are well-known: A pious and musical shepherd boy fearlessly battles and tri-
umphs over an overlarge foe named Goliath and becomes Israel's greatest
king. Though David is far from perfect—there is that little matter with Bathsheba, for example (2 Sam. 11)—he nonetheless is remembered as the man
after God's own heart.[1]

For many modern readers, the mere mention of David and love might also
call to mind a particular relationship: namely, his relationship with Jonathan,
the firstborn son of Saul, the first king of Israel. Though I briefly mention Jonathan here, I leave the full exploration of David and Jonathan's relationship
for the following chapter. Here instead, I focus on David's relationship not
with Jonathan but with Jonathan's father, Saul, and the ways in which love is
imagined in the stories of these two figures. Not only does Saul's interaction
and relationship with David establish the context for David's relationship with
Jonathan but the stories about Saul also most effectively and fully reveal the
multivalent and complex meanings of love, especially as love interacts with
fate and divine preference.

---

1. Mark K. George, "Yhwh's Own Heart," *Catholic Biblical Quarterly* 64, no. 3 (2002):
442–59. I will posit a different understanding of the man-after-God's-own-heart than the one
proposed by George.

In particular, like Jacob and Esau, so also Saul, the divinely rejected and unloved, is contrasted to David, the divinely favored and beloved. Divine preference or rejection, which is related to parental favoritism, is the key factor that determines whether a character receives or loses the love of other characters. We have, with Esau, already seen how divine choice affects the unloved and unpreferred. However, Saul differs from Esau in the clarity of God's rejection, the severity of repercussions that ensues, and the degree of God's involvement in bringing about these results. While God seemed happy to remain on the sidelines during the mistreatment of Esau, in Saul's case, God plays a more active and calculating role in the rise of Saul to kingship and his eventual fall from power. In short, the story of Saul and David portrays God as deliberately setting Saul up to fail, and in so doing, portrays God as vastly crueler and more unfair than in the previous story of Jacob and Esau.

If love is intertwined with God, as I argued in the previous chapter, this problematic portrayal of God as reflected in the pathos of Saul further pushes the contours of how love should be imagined. Namely, by focusing on the central question—why does God, with his preference, create a situation where Saul loses his crown to David, the first and only person Saul is said to love (1 Sam. 16:21)?—I propose that God's harsh reactions to Saul is caused by his own heartbreak and unrequited love. Love's power is so great that even God is depicted as its victim.

THE LOVE OF DAVID

Unknown to most, the first character in the biblical text to state that they love (*ahav*) David is Saul, the first king of Israel (1 Sam. 16:21). Shortly after Saul's rejection as king, David enters Saul's service as a musician to soothe Saul's affliction of an evil spirit and thereby gains his favor. Saul's love of David is quickly followed by the love of many others (1 Sam. 16:21; 18:1, 3, 16, 20, 22, 28; 20:17). David is so irresistible in fact that, barring all but the most reviled characters—such as Nabal, whose name means "fool" and who is swiftly dispatched by God after his disrespectful treatment of David in 1 Sam. 25[2]—nearly all who see David fall victim to his charisma and, as we will see, come

2. There are many articles and essays on the story of Abigail, Nabal, and David. See e.g., Adele Berlin, "Characterization in Biblical Narrative: David's Wives," *Journal for the Study of the Old Testament* 23 (1982): 69–85; Marjorie O'Rourke Boyle, "The Law of the Heart: The Death of a Fool (1 Samuel 25)," *Journal of Biblical Literature* 120, no. 3 (2001): 401–27; Samuel Ben-Meir, "Nabal, the Villain," *Jewish Bible Quarterly* 22 (1994): 249–51; Jon D. Levenson, "1 Samuel 25 as Literature and as History," *Catholic Biblical Quarterly* 40, no. 1 (1978): 11–28; Ellen van Wolde, "A Leader Led by a Lady: David and Abigail in I Samuel 25," *Zeitschrift für die alttestamentliche Wissenschaft* 114, no. 3 (2002): 355–75.

to mysteriously and irrationally love him: all of Israel and Judah, especially its armies (1 Sam. 18:16), and all of Saul's servants (1 Sam. 18:22) are said to love David. Especially afflicted is the family of Saul, who go crazy over this new addition to the court. Jonathan, the firstborn son of Saul, is said several times to love David (1 Sam. 18:1, 3; 20:17), while Michal, Jonathan's sister, who is depicted as similar to Jonathan, also falls under David's spell, so much so that she ends up marrying him (1 Sam. 18:20, 27–28).

Yet knowing what eventually happens to Saul and his family, especially those who come to love David (hint: nothing good), this love is striking and odd. Considering that David eventually replaces Saul as king, it is especially strange that Saul is said to be the *first* to love David. Saul will suffer the most for this love of David, eventually losing his crown, his life, and his dynasty to the upstart. Hence, Saul should be the last or the least likely to love David, not the first. Why is the first king of Israel depicted as the first to love the man who will eventually come to usurp him? What is the purpose of this fatal attraction, as it were, and what does it say about love?

As these questions make clear, Saul is undoubtedly central to David's story. Because David comes to replace Saul as king, their relationship, their destiny, and the love that is present, obtained, and lost between them are deeply and intimately intertwined. Without Saul, there is no David—at least not the one we know through the biblical text—and without the rejection of Saul, there is no selection and love of David. As with the oppositional twins, Esau and Jacob, there can be no winner without a loser. Their intertwined relationship not only heightens the tragedy of their story, especially that of Saul,[3] but also reveals the theological, political, familial, societal, and emotional importance and effects of love—a love that, as the stories about Saul show, emerges directly from the mysterious whims and preferences of God.

As this chapter will explore, the key reason why Saul, his family, and everyone else is depicted as so quick to fall in love with David is so that his rise, and therefore Saul's downfall, can be portrayed as something fated, divinely ordained, and unstoppable. The reason these events are fated, these stories show, is because David's rise comes from and is driven by God's mysterious preference for David, a preference that causes everyone around him to inexplicably love him. The connection between divine preference and love is directly acknowledged by the text: "Saul saw and knew that the LORD was

---

3. On Saul's story as tragedy, see W. Lee Humphreys, "The Tragedy of King Saul: A Study of the Structure of 1 Samuel 9–31," *Journal for the Study of the Old Testament* 6 (1978): 18–27; Humphreys, "The Rise and Fall of King Saul: A Study of an Ancient Narrative Stratum in 1 Samuel," *Journal for the Study of the Old Testament* 8 (1980): 74–90; Humphreys, "From Tragic Hero to Villain: A Study of the Figure of Saul and the Development of 1 Samuel," *Journal for the Study of the Old Testament* 22 (1982): 95–117.

with David, and that all of Israel loved him" (1 Sam. 18:28).[4] Though the text
never directly states that God loved David, 1 Samuel 18:28 clearly stresses that
divine preference induces and is connected to the love (*ahav*) David receives
from other characters, including Saul.[5] Indeed, Saul is depicted as the first
to love David, in part because David is hired to help with Saul's affliction of
the evil spirit (1 Sam. 16:14–23). As such, Saul is the first to recognize and
experience God's preference for David as it is related to his own loss of divine
preference as manifested in his spiritual affliction.

This divinely induced love is so powerful that it acts as a magnet for other
things, such as power, loyalty, acumen, and success, thereby facilitating David's
rise. This love is also so irresistible that even those who pay the ultimate price
for it, such as Saul and members of his family, cannot help but fall victim to
it. By showing how David's rise is fated and divinely ordained, the downfall
of Saul and his family, in contrast, can also be excused away as the unfortunate but ultimately unavoidable effects of love—a love that emanates from
the inexplicable and whimsical preferences of God, a deity who, for reasons
that I will try to elucidate later, has decided to reject Saul and favor David. By
miring God's preferences in mystery and secrecy, David's role in the demise
of Saul and his family and the usurpation of his throne is also obfuscated. It is
God and God's preferences, in inducing or inhibiting love, and *not certain people*
who are therefore ultimately to blame for the regime change, civil war, and
murders that follow.

THE DIVINE SELECTION OF SAUL

For a reign that will end so badly, readers might be surprised to learn that
Saul is chosen to become Israel's first monarch not once, but three times
in three separate accounts. In the first account, Saul goes in search of
errant donkeys only to encounter the prophet Samuel, who is directed by
God to anoint Saul as king (1 Sam. 9:15–17). This account is followed by
a second, less dramatic account at 1 Samuel 10:17–27, which tells of how
Saul became king after being selected by Samuel who uses lots—a kind of
sacred dice—to choose the first king of Israel. Finally, in the last account

---

4. This is the English translation following the Septuagint (LXX). The Masoretic Text
(MT) instead states, "Saul saw and knew that the Lord was with David, and that indeed
Michal, the daughter of Saul, loved him" (my own translation). In either case, God's preference
for David is depicted as connected to the love of David by other human characters.

5. God is only said to love two kings, Solomon (2 Sam. 12:24–25) and Cyrus (Isa. 48:14).
Usually, instead of directly stating God loves someone, the biblical text instead states that God
chooses, selects, or is with someone, such as David (1 Sam. 16:1; 18:14, 28).

at 1 Samuel 11:1–15, in a story that harkens back to the devastating tale about
the rape and dismemberment of a Levite's concubine that concludes the book
of Judges (Judg. 19–21), Saul summons an army and rescues a town called
Jabesh-Gilead from a foreign enemy and is crowned monarch.[6]

The multiplicity of accounts of Saul's enthronement might be initially mis-
read as signs of reaffirmation. Instead, when carefully examined, they bespeak
God's lack of enthusiasm and, likely, of love for the newly chosen monarch.
Like a romance that will end in a nasty divorce, there are already signs, even
in the accounts of Saul's enthronement, that things will go terribly awry—or
to use the marriage metaphor, that this "marriage" will be short-lived and that
a divorce is simply a matter of time. The text presages the coming "divorce"
between Saul and God by depicting even their honeymoon period as, at best,
dismal and ambivalent.

The order of the three stories of Saul's coronation suggests that Saul's selection as king was a divine mistake, one which God wants quietly and quickly
to walk back or rectify.[7] As we move from the first to the last story of Saul's
enthronement, God appears increasingly less involved and increasingly less
confident in the selection and choice of Saul. For example, in the first story
where Saul goes in search of lost animals, God clearly and adamantly chooses
Saul, identifying to Samuel, the prophet, both the date of Saul's appearance (1
Sam. 19:15–16) as well as the man himself when Saul happens to stumble into
town: "When Samuel saw Saul, the LORD told him, 'Here is the man of whom
I spoke to you. He it is who shall rule over my people'" (1 Sam. 9:17). God's
selection of Saul as king the first time is also affirmed by several additional
signs (1 Sam. 10:1–8) and certified in 1 Samuel 10:9, which states that "God
gave him [Saul] another heart."

God's choice of Saul seems generally clear and unequivocal in the first
story. However, even in this story, which is the most affirmative of the three,
doubts and questions are raised. Like a partner who cannot give a clear reason for the marriage, God never explains *why* Saul was chosen to become

6. On the polemic against Saul in the book of Judges, see Yairah Amit, *Hidden Polemics in the Biblical Narrative*, trans. Jonathan Chipman, Biblical Interpretation Series 25 (Leiden: Brill, 2000), esp. 178–88; Yairah Amit, "Literature in the Service of Politics: Studies in Judges 19–21," in *Politics and Theopolitics in the Bible and Postbiblical Literature*, ed. Henning Graf Reventlow, Yair Hoffman, and Benjamin Uffenheimer, Journal for the Study of the Old Testament Supplement Series 171 (Sheffield: Sheffield Academic, 1994), 28–40; Marc Zvi Brettler, *The Book of Judges*, Old Testament Readings (London: Routledge, 2001), 412–18; Suzie Park, "Left-Handed Benjaminites and the Shadow of Saul," *Journal of Biblical Literature* 134, no. 4 (2015): 701–20; Marvin A. Sweeney, "Davidic Polemics in the Book of Judges," *Vetus Testamentum* 47, fasc. 4 (1997): 517–29.

7. On causation in the stories of the accession of King Saul, see Rachelle Gilmour, *Representing the Past: A Literary Analysis of Narrative Historiography in the Book of Samuel* (Leiden: Brill, 2011), esp. 63–72.

Israel's king in the first place. Saul himself expresses confusion over his selection, questioning and asking Samuel when he is selected, saying, "I am only a Benjaminite, from the least of the tribes of Israel, and my family is the humblest of all the families of the tribe of Benjamin. Why then have you spoken to me in this way?" (9:21). Not only does Saul's confusion, aside from portraying himself as an underdog,[8] reflect the confusion of the readers, but more disturbingly, neither God nor Samuel has a good answer for Saul. No one seems to know why God chose Saul as king.

Tellingly, as the reader moves through the three stories of Saul's selection as king—lost donkeys to lots to military rescue—God's preference for Saul as the first king becomes increasingly less emphatic, less clear, and therefore less certain. So much so that, in contrast to the first story, by the third and last story, God is not even really involved in the selection of Saul as king (1 Sam. 11:1–15). Instead, it is the people, not God, who choose and crown Saul as king after they realize that he is an effective military leader and able to rouse and gather the requisite forces needed to fend off Israel's enemies.

By having the three stories of Saul's ascent progressively less pronounced and less emphatic as to God's role in the selection of Saul as king, the narrative seems to walk back this event. By obscuring how exactly Saul came to be in this position in the first place and therefore, relatedly, the role God had in it, so also obscured is God's choice of Saul as the first king of Israel. By having three different stories of Saul's anointment, some of which emphasize God's role in the selection of Saul as the first king, the overall sentiment is that it was a combination of unknowable forces—everything from divine choice or divine passive assent to military and political skill or societal need and change or simply dumb luck on the part of Saul—that led to him becoming the first king.

This blurring not only helps to somewhat decrease the number of disturbing theological questions about God and God's preferences—namely, aside from cruelty and boredom, why did God choose Saul to become king only to reject him soon after?—but most importantly, it strongly hints that Saul's kingship is doomed to fail. Not clearly chosen by God, at least, not in all the stories, there are questions about how bona fide or sanctioned Saul's reign really is. Adding to the doubts, in no story of Saul's coronation is anyone ever said to love Saul. And this lack of love can be contrasted to the robust love that David, the next king, receives when he arrives on the scene. As such, this lack of love signals that God is not alone in having regrets, and in hindsight there were always doubts about Saul's kingship and whether it was a good idea in the first place.

---

8. Susan Niditch, *A Prelude to Biblical Folklore: Underdogs and Tricksters* (San Francisco: Harper & Row, 1987).

THE DIVINE REJECTION OF SAUL

Aside from obfuscating the role of God in the selection of Saul as king, the narrative also accentuates Saul's offenses so as to show the inevitability of Saul's downfall and therefore the inevitability of David's rise. Just as quickly as Saul becomes king, he is rejected by God as king. Immediately after the three stories of Saul's anointment, two subsequent stories describe two mistakes or misdeeds on the part of Saul that lead to his rejection by God and his replacement by David.

The first story tells of how Saul, before one of the battles, fails to wait long enough for the prophet Samuel to arrive and perform the sacrifice (1 Sam. 13). Seeing impatient soldiers leaving before the start of a battle and having waited the requisite number of days stated by the prophet Samuel (1 Sam. 13:8), Saul offers the burnt offering himself (1 Sam. 13:9). Suspiciously, just as Saul finishes the sacrifice, Samuel shows up, admonishes him, and then tells him that as a result of his misdeed the Lord will now seek a man "after his own heart" to be appointed ruler instead (1 Sam. 13:13–14). The term "heart" (*lev/levav*), as I will discuss later in this chapter, is a dense term with a complex meaning in Hebrew.

This story is followed two chapters later by another that describes a second offense by Saul, which is similarly unclear, and which heightens the mystery of divine rejection. In the second story, Saul is commanded by God to battle and put the Amalekites under the ban (1 Sam. 15). The ban, or *herem*, was a type of holy war whereby enemy groups were attacked and everything destroyed as a sacrifice to the Lord, including animals and children.[9] Saul follows through with God's commands, attacking the Amalekites and destroying nearly everything belonging to them. However, instead of destroying everything immediately, he spares the Amalekite king and some of the best animals in order to sacrifice them at a later celebration (1 Sam. 15:8–9).

Saul again is bedeviled by problems of interpretation and communication. Apparently what Saul did was the very thing he was not supposed to do, and Samuel again shows up to confront Saul about disobeying his instructions (1 Sam. 15:13–23). As in the first story, the prophet finishes his harangue in the second story by again telling Saul that, because of Saul's mistake, God has rejected him as king and will therefore give his kingdom to another: "And Samuel said to him, 'The LORD has torn the kingdom of Israel from you this very day, and has given it to a neighbor of yours, who is better than you'" (1 Sam. 15:28). Considering the doubt exhibited during Saul's enthronement, it

---

9. Susan Niditch, *War in the Hebrew Bible: A Study in the Ethics of Violence* (New York: Oxford University Press, 1993).

is hard to shake the feeling that God, regretful of the earlier decision with Saul, is using technicalities related to timing to start arguments so as to find a way out of a relationship with Saul.

A sense of increasing dissatisfaction lends support to this idea. The story of Saul's second misdeed (1 Sam. 15) exacerbates the questions and confusion that are present in the first story (1 Sam. 13). Namely, the first story leaves unclear the nature of Saul's mistake, and why Saul's action was so bad as to warrant such a heavy punishment: the loss of his reign. The second story increases the intensity of these questions. As in the first story, we are again not told what exactly Saul did wrong. However, in the second account, both God and Samuel imply that Saul did something egregious, something very, very bad indeed. God charges Saul with "turn[ing] back from following" God and failing to carry out God's commandments (1 Sam. 15:11), and Samuel likens Saul's misdeed to rebellion, divination, and idolatry (1 Sam. 15:23). Saul's deed—whatever it might be—is so offensive that Samuel rebuffs Saul's numerous attempts to repent of his mysterious mistake (1 Sam. 15:20–21, 24–26, 30–31).

The emotional effects of this rejection add to the confusion. Not only is Samuel angry (1 Sam. 15:11) and aggrieved (15:35), but Saul, who will pay the highest price for God's rejection, reacts with despair and terror. Saul tries to apologize three times, only to be rebuffed by Samuel each time. The number of times Saul apologizes, tellingly, is the number of times he was selected as king. Judging by Saul's apologies, which lack detail, Saul seems confused as to what he did wrong but is desperate to make amends anyway. Speaking to Saul's increasing distress and frustration (1 Sam. 15:20, 24–25, 30)—he even tries to bar Samuel from leaving until they have reconciled, holding on to the hem of Samuel's robe to the point of it tearing—is something that the prophet uses as a sign-act to confirm God's rejection of Saul and his reign (1 Sam. 15:27–28). The final, desperate pleading by Saul bespeaks his sorrow and heartbreak, and hints of Saul's awareness of the devastating effects of divine rejection, as exemplified by the loss of Samuel's support: a loss of love and with it, the loss of power, loyalty, and ultimately his life. As these characters' reactions to the divine rejection show, the breakup and the cessation of love that follows from it causes not only material loss but emotional havoc for all involved.

This second story of Saul's rejection undoubtedly raises the dramatic stakes. Increasing the emotions as well as the magnitude of Saul's misdeed, this story exacerbates the confusion over Saul's mistake and, therefore, the confusion over God's reasons for the rejection of Saul: What exactly did Saul do wrong? That is, what could Saul possibly have done that is so horrific, so unforgivable, that even after multiple apologies it leads God to regret that he made Saul king in the first place? It surely cannot simply be that Saul incorrectly interpreted Samuel's instructions? Indeed, if the offense was so terrible, why is Saul's mistake not described more clearly?[10]

These questions might be the point. That is, there is no good reason that can explain or justify why Saul, who is chosen by God as king a few chapters earlier (1 Sam. 9–11), is suddenly rejected as king by the same God (1 Sam. 13, 15). By leaving Saul's misdeeds unclear, by emphasizing that Saul did something bad, and by portraying these mistakes as unforgivable, the narrative points to and even stresses the lack of answers—the lack of a reason—behind Saul's rejection. In so doing, through the unclarity and confusion, the narrative suggests that Saul's fall is simply a matter of fate, simply due to God's whims. Indeed, the question—what did Saul do wrong to lose his kingship?—is the wrong question. It is a diversion tactic used to obscure the fact that Saul loses God's favoritism and therefore his kingship without reason, simply because it was destined. That is, because God, whose preferences are random, mysterious, and unstable, appears to have decreed it be so. Saul's downfall and therefore David's rise, though inexplicable, again are therefore shown to be inevitable—and this incontrovertibly, as I will explain, affects the understanding of love.

THE HEAVY HAND OF GOD

That God has it out for Saul for some mysterious reason, thereby making his downfall inevitable, is evident in the active role that God has in bringing about his fate. God throws every obstacle in the path of Saul as he tries to hold on to his power. In contrast, God does everything he can to aid the usurper, David. While Saul is still on the throne, God promptly sets to work by getting David, his new favorite, crowned king. Immediately after Saul's misdeed, God, rather quick in getting over Saul, commands Samuel to stop grieving for the hapless first monarch and go appoint a new king in Saul's place (1 Sam. 16:1). Ever obedient, Samuel promptly does so, secretly and treasonously anointing David while Saul is still in power (16:13).

Though I will later propose a possible rationale behind God's rapidly changing preferences, which are never spelled out in the text, there are signs

---

10. On the confusion and perhaps divine hostility behind Saul's rejection, see J. Cheryl Exum, *Tragedy and Biblical Narrative* (Cambridge, UK: Cambridge University Press, 1992), esp. 41; David M. Gunn, *The Fate of King Saul: An Interpretation of a Biblical Story* (Sheffield: JSOT Press, 1980), 33–58, 131. On an interesting interpretation of Saul's mistakes as being overly righteous, see Rachelle Gilmour, "Saul's Rejection and the Obscene Underside of the Law," *The Bible and Critical Theory* 15, no. 1 (2019): 34–45.

that, in contrast to Saul, David's kingship will be more successful. Not only is David described as handsome and ruddy, signifying his virility and military talent—necessary masculine traits of all successful ancient Near Eastern kings—but he is also portrayed as an underdog.[11] David is such an underdog that, while his father is parading all of his brothers in front of Samuel when the prophet arrives to anoint a new king, David is out herding sheep (1 Sam. 16:6–12). Considering that being an underdog as well as a shepherd signals future leaders in the ancient Near East, David, from the very beginning, is depicted as a man destined to be king.[12] God seems to have improved at picking monarchs the second time around.

The problem, however, is that God has yet to completely undo the mistake of his first selection. Though God has rejected Saul, he still remains on the throne. And God, for some reason, decides to take the scenic route when it comes to the removal of the first king. Aside from anointing David as king while Saul is still alive, God helps David (and hampers Saul) by switching hearts (*levav*) and spirits (*ruah*). First Samuel 16:7 emphasizes David's possession of this mysterious, divinely desired heart:[13] "the LORD does not see as mortals see; they look on the outward appearance, but the LORD looks on the heart." This statement again depicts David as an underdog and contrasts him to Saul who is tall and therefore only *looks* the part of a king (1 Sam. 9:2). More importantly, the reference to David's heart alludes to Samuel's comment to Saul in the first rejection story that God will seek a "man after his own heart" to be made ruler in Saul's place (1 Sam. 13:13–14). The message is clear: though David does not look like much, he is king where it really counts—in the heart. In contrast, Saul therefore must lack this heart or have the wrong kind.

Yet what about the new appropriate heart given to Saul right after his coronation at 1 Samuel 10:9—"God gave him [Saul] another heart"? What happened to it? Though the text does not say, considering the contrast between David and Saul, and considering the effects of divine rejection, which are the

11. Scott B. Noegel, "Scarlets and Harlots: Seeing Red in the Hebrew Bible," *Hebrew Union College Annual* 87 (2016): 31; Cynthia R. Chapman, *The Gendered Language of Warfare in the Israelite-Assyrian Encounter*, Harvard Semitic Monographs 62 (Winona Lake: Eisenbrauns, 2004), esp. 20–59, 83; Ovidiu Creangă, ed., *Men and Masculinity in the Hebrew Bible* (Sheffield: Sheffield Phoenix Press, 2010); Deborah W. Rooke, ed., *A Question of Sex? Gender and Difference in the Hebrew Bible and Beyond* (Sheffield: Sheffield Phoenix Press, 2007); Steven L. McKenzie, *King David: A Biography* (New York: Oxford University Press, 2000), 70.

12. McKenzie, *King David*, 47–50.

13. For a different understanding of David's "heart" as indicative of his religiosity, see George, "Yhwh's Own Heart," 442–59. Moreover, for "heart" as a mysterious quality desired by God, see Benjamin Johnson, "The Heart of the Chosen One in 1 Samuel," *Journal of Biblical Literature* 131, no. 3 (2012): 455–66.

opposite of divine selection and favoritism, the assumption here is that the hearts have been switched. (As I will discuss, along with the hearts, the spirits [*ruah*] also appear to have been switched.) That is, David, as God's newly favored and selected, and therefore newly crowned, has received an appropriate heart for the task. Poor Saul, in contrast, as God's newly rejected and therefore about to be de-crowned, must have lost the heart that he received when he was coronated. Bespeaking the broken love, Saul's heart is no more. Rather, it has been given to David.

Aside from emphasizing David and Saul as opposites—the divinely favored and the divinely rejected—a feature we saw with Esau and Jacob as well, the switch or replacement of hearts reflects God's hand in bringing about the fates: that is, the success of the favored and the failure of the unfavored. This is evident in the complicated meanings of "heart" (*levav*) in the Hebrew text. While "heart" (*levav*) in modern Western understanding is viewed as the seat of emotions, in the Hebrew text it is "primarily the locus of reason, intelligence, of secret planning, deliberation, and decision" (Deut. 29:4; 1 Sam. 14:7; Isa. 10:7; 63:4).[14] That is, though the "heart" is associated with senses, emotions, and affections in the Hebrew Bible as well (Pss. 73:21; 104:15; 109:16; Prov. 5:12; 31:11; Eccl. 2:20), the biblical text also views it as the seat of activity and conduct (Deut. 6:4–5).[15] Emotions and actions, as I discussed in an earlier chapter, are coterminous and not easily separated in the Hebrew text.

Hence, applying this definition of "heart" to the story of Saul and David, I would take "heart" to mean a kind of political know-how, acumen, and emotional balance needed to be a successful king. As such, the recognition or gain of heart by David, the likely cause and result of divine preference, suggests that God has both recognized and possibly even augmented David's political acumen and mental sensibilities. In contrast, the loss of heart by Saul, the effect of divine rejection, means that God has hampered and debilitated Saul's political and emotional abilities—his wisdom, decision-making abilities, mental balance, and planning skills. The oppositional maneuverings of the heart, which stems from God's changing preferences, therefore, reflect divine maneuvers to give God's newly favored a leg up in the competition to take the throne; and in contrast, to give God's newly rejected a better chance to lose it by (to continue the leg metaphor) kneecapping him. As such, the use of "heart" stresses the contrast between the unloved, rejected Saul and the

---

14. Thomas Staubli and Silvia Schroer, *Body Symbolism in the Bible*, trans. Linda M. Maloney (Collegeville, MN: Liturgical Press, 2001), 43.

15. Andreas Schuele, "Heart," in *The New Interpreter's Dictionary of the Bible*, vol. 2, ed. Katharine Doob Sakenfeld (Nashville, TN: Abingdon, 2007), 764–66.

beloved, favored David. No wonder David's name, from the Hebrew *dod*, can mean beloved.[16]

God does not stop with the heart, however. Another prompt consequence of divine selection and rejection, which hastens Saul's downfall and David's ascent, is the movement of the *ruah*, which is usually translated as spirit, and which connotes breath, divine presence, spirit, animus, human life, or even simply wind in the Hebrew text.[17] As with Saul, who experiences the rushing upon of the Lord's spirit shortly after he is appointed king (1 Sam. 11:6), immediately after David's secret anointment, 1 Samuel 16:13 states, "Then Samuel took the horn of oil, and anointed him [David] . . . . and the spirit of the LORD came mightily upon David from that day forward." This movement of the spirit on David is matched by the opposite movement of the spirit for Saul: "Now the spirit of the LORD departed from Saul, and an evil spirit from the LORD tormented him" (1 Sam. 16:14).

Considering the various meanings of spirit, *ruah*, a good spirit seems to entail a kind of luck, energy, and harmony of body and mind that comes from God's favor. In contrast, a bad *ruah* appears to entail the opposite: bad luck, a lack of energy, and, as we will see, even physical and mental discomfort of some sort—the feeling that one is out of sorts with the world, and in this case, with God. *Ruah*, in short, connotes activity—in the case of Saul and David, God's actions and activity. Indeed, according to Thomas Staubli and Silvia Schroer, *ruah* "is always active, producing dynamism," it "creates room, puts in motion, leads out of narrowness into broad space, and gives life" (Gen. 1:2; Ps. 104:29–30).[18] As such, considering that both spirits are said to be from or of the Lord, and considering that this switching of *ruah* occurs right after David's secret anointment as king, this movement is another consequence of divine selection and, its opposite, divine rejection. Moreover, considering the *ruah* entails activity and action, the switching of divine spirits, like the heart, seems to entail divine actions that hasten God's desired results: namely, the rise of David and the downfall of Saul.

Finally, as if all these maneuvers were not enough, God speeds up the desired conclusion by using the spirits to land David in the exact right position to take over Saul's throne. Because of divine rejection, the (presumably good) spirit of the Lord moves from Saul to David and is replaced with an evil spirit

16. The Hebrew word *dod*, which underlies the name "David," is paralleled to *ahav* (Prov. 7:18) and can mean beloved, especially in the Song of Songs, which uses this term extensively (Song 1:2; 2:8–10, 13–14, 16). More often, however, it means "uncle" or "friend" (Lev. 10:4, 20:20, 25:49; Num. 36:11; 1 Sam. 10:14–16, 14:50; 2 Kgs. 24:17). The latter meaning, in the case of David, is ironic.

17. John R. Levison, "Holy Spirit," in *New Interpreter's Dictionary of the Bible*, vol. 2, ed. Katharine Doob Sakenfeld (Nashville: Abingdon, 2007), 859–79.

18. Staubli and Schroer, *Body Symbolism in the Bible*, 214.

from the Lord (1 Sam. 16:14), which causes Saul to be mysteriously afflict-ed.[19] Though the exact nature of Saul's spiritual affliction is unclear, Saul, because of this sickness, looks for a musician who can soothe him and is rec-ommended David by one of his servants: "One of the young men answered, 'I have seen a son of Jesse the Bethlehemite who is skillful in playing, a man of valor, a warrior, prudent in speech, and a man of good presence; and the LORD is with him'" (1 Sam. 16:18).[20]

This description of David by Saul's servant, which is rich in subtext, again hints that David is divinely ordained to take the throne from Saul. Not only is David's entire résumé offered here, but the qualities listed by the servant go far beyond what is needed for a part-time music therapist. Especially impor-tant is the mention of David's music skills. Considering that music is linked to the prophetic, otherworldly, divine, or magical,[21] his aptitude implies that David is spiritually gifted or divinely favored. This description also indicates that David, unlike Saul, is better able to communicate with God. Considering that communication, especially with God, is the very thing that foils Saul both times when he misinterprets Samuel's directions, this description of David contrasts him favorably over against Saul.[22] Indeed, the servant's recommen-dation emphasizes how David has all the exact right qualities needed to be a successful monarch—that is, David can fight ("man of valor" and "good warrior"), is divinely favored ("skillful in playing [music]" and "the LORD is with him"), and politically astute ("prudent in speech").[23] As I show in the next chapter, these qualities are the very ones that are said to be lacking for Saul.

---

19. On Saul's spiritual affliction, see H. C. Ackerman, "Saul: A Psychotherapeutic Analysis," *Anglican Theological Review* 3, no. 2 (1920): 114–24; Liubov Ben-Noun, "What Was the Mental Disease That Afflicted Saul?," *Clinical Case Studies* 2 no. 4 (2003): 270–82; Philip Francis Esler, "The Madness of Saul: A Cultural Reading of 1 Samuel 8–31," in *Biblical Studies/Cultural Studies*, ed. J. Cheryl Exum and Stephen D. Moore (Sheffield: Sheffield Academic Press, 1998), 220–62; Staubli and Schroer, *Body Symbolism*, 217; Gillian Patricia Williams and Magdel Le Roux, "King Saul's Mysterious Malady," *Hervormde teologiese studies* 68, no. 1 (2012): 1–6. On an examination of each of David's features, see McKenzie, *King David*, 51–66.

20. On an examination of each of David's features, see McKenzie, *King David*, 51–66.

21. McKenzie writes, "In the ancient world, music served more of a religious and magical function. It played an important role in the temple worship . . . . It was also used to induce pro-phetic trances . . . David's strumming on the lyre was meant to relieve Saul from the tortures of the evil spirit sent from Yahweh. But this was not just because of its soothing sound. Music was believed to possess magical powers to keep away or exorcise demons and evil spirits. David was a magician as much as a musician" (*King David*, 56). On the significance of heightened speech, such as songs, see Song-Mi Suzie Park, "The Frustration of Wisdom: Wisdom, Counsel, and Divine Will in 2 Samuel 17:1–23," *Journal of Biblical Literature* 128, no. 3 (2009): 453–67.

22. This problem of divine miscommunication will continue to hamper Saul. So much so that before his final battle, he is forced to consult a necromancer (1 Sam. 28).

23. McKenzie, *King David*, 51–66. For David's story as propaganda and apology, see P. Kyle McCarter, "The Apology of David," *Journal of Biblical Literature* 99, no. 4 (1980): 489–504;

Hence, in a cruel twist, God afflicts Saul with an evil spirit and then uses it to land David in the exact right place to usurp his throne. Like an intern who eventually becomes CEO, this entrance into the royal court gives David the opportunity to get close to the center of power, the king himself. In so doing, it allows David—in modern parlance—to gain hands-on experience, networking opportunities, and insider knowledge of the intricate workings and structure of Israel's political system. Saul's affliction, therefore, offers David an opportunity to take the initial steps to becoming king. Like the person who, ignorant of their upcoming firing, unwittingly trains their own replacement, the person whom Saul obtains to relieve him from God's affliction happens to be the very one mysteriously chosen by God to precipitate his downfall.

THE POWER OF LOVE

This troubling context forms the background to the first mention of love in the stories about David and Saul and, as such, reveals how love is imagined in these narratives. Right after David's entrance into court as a musician to help ease Saul's illness, 1 Samuel 16:21–23 states that Saul shortly came to love and depend on David:

> And David came to Saul, and entered his service. Saul loved [*ahav*] him greatly, and he became his armor-bearer. Saul sent to Jesse, saying, "Let David remain in my service, for he has found favor in my sight." And whenever the evil spirit from God came upon Saul, David took the lyre and played it with his hand, and Saul would be relieved and feel better, and the evil spirit would depart from him. (1 Sam. 16:21–23)

The first detail we notice with this description is the astonishing effect of God's preference. As I noted earlier, this preference seems to be the key determining factor as to whether a character wins or loses the love of other characters. It is so influential that, according to 1 Samuel 16:21, even Saul—the divinely rejected and divinely set up—cannot help but come to love David even though this love will cost him and his family everything. As the story makes clear, love, which follows from the powerful and mercurial preference of God, is just as powerful—and just as mercurial. The magnitude and capriciousness of love manifest in its double-sided nature. Capable of bringing loyalty, luck, astuteness, mental wellbeing, influence, and even relationships, love

---

P. Kyle McCarter, "The Historical David," *Interpretation* 40, no. 2 (1986): 117–29; Keith Whitelam, "The Defence of David," *Journal for the Study of the Old Testament* 29 (1984): 61–87.

can repel these things as well. With love's loss so also lost are things essential to one's well-being and, more importantly, within this literary context, to one's survival. Considering love's potency, the statement about Saul's love of David at 1 Samuel 16:21 therefore cannot be taken as anything short of a premature publication of Saul's obituary.

Saul's slow downfall, which begins at the moment he meets and comes to love David, is full of pathos and feeling. As with the story of Jacob and Esau, the biblical text draws out and lingers on the weight and appalling cost—emotional, familial, societal, and political—of Saul's love. Hinting at familial ramifications, Saul is said to love David, so much so that he takes him into the family, treating him almost like an adopted son (1 Sam. 16:21–22). Considering that Saul is never said to love any of his children, including his firstborn son, Jonathan (a failure which, as the next chapter reveals, has immense consequences), the statement of Saul's love and quasi-adoption of David reveals a striking level of trust, vulnerability, and closeness. Saul appears to feel a sense of affinity, of kinship, with David—perhaps even more so than with members of his own family.[24] All of this heightens the tragic nature of Saul's story and, in so doing, unveils love's (and God's) darker side.

Perhaps the cruelest consequence of love centers on Saul's spiritual affliction. The mention of Saul's love for David and his desire for his presence along with descriptions of David's effectiveness in providing relief at 1 Samuel 16:23 strongly implies these things are connected. Saul's love of David, in short, is tightly bound up with Saul's need for David as a source of pain alleviation and as a caregiver. Indeed, it is likely not coincidence that David is the first person whom Saul is said to love. Considering that David appears at a particularly vulnerable time for Saul, offering a measure of relief no less, this expression of affection is hardly surprising.

The omniscient reader knows, of course, that this is all part of God's long-term plan to replace Saul with David. Despite this knowledge, however, Saul's reliance on David also speaks to their complicated relationship, and in so far as love is mentioned, complicates the idea of love, especially as love intersects with power and politics. Though Saul is king, considering that he is dependent on David and his musical abilities to assuage his affliction, it is unclear who is the more powerful of the two. There are strong hints in fact—the double rejection of Saul (1 Sam. 13, 15), the secret coronation of David (1 Sam.

---

24. David too seems to feel a sense of affinity of sorts with Saul in so far as David wants to take over and be in Saul's position. Moreover, this statement of Saul's love and quasi-adoption, especially in a context in which families are central, undoubtedly is used to justify David's usurpation. What David does is not a usurpation, the text implies. Rather, David is family, and his coronation is merely the next step, a logical upgrade of his familial status as a part of the royal family.

16:13), the mention of the heart (1 Sam. 13:14; 16:7), the numerous factions that love David (1 Sam. 16:21; 18:1, 16, 20, 28; 20:17), and the switching of the spirit (1 Sam. 16:14)—that indicate that the social and power hierarchy is not as it initially appears. Though Saul, as king, is technically politically and socially of higher standing than David, it is really David who has the upper hand. As God says, "Do not look on his appearance or on the height of his stature . . . for the LORD does not see as mortals see; they look on the outward appearance, but the LORD looks on the heart" (1 Sam. 16:7).

If Saul, the one who loves, is depicted here as the weaker, less powerful party, then Saul's love of David hints that love has to entail some amount of vulnerability and dependency as well as a loss of or renegotiation of power. Tellingly, though 1 Samuel 16:21 states that Saul loved David, the text never states that David loved Saul or anyone else for that matter. The lack of reciprocity not only speaks to David's lack of loyalty to Saul, but it also stresses the dangers of love.[25] That is, God places Saul in an impossible situation: Saul needs to feel better from his affliction—one which God intentionally causes to hasten Saul's dethronement; however, to feel better, Saul needs the services of the very person who will dethrone him.[26] Saul, despite being king, needs David and is therefore in a position of relative weakness. David, in contrast, has little need of Saul. Indeed, while Saul needs David's presence, David, who likely has royal aspirations, desires the opposite, Saul's absence. Hence, Saul has to love David, but David does not have to, and indeed does not love Saul. Love, therefore, is portrayed as dangerous, capable of causing pain and possibly even death.

Saul's affliction, his love for David, and his cure at the hands of his usurper should make us wonder why God puts Saul in such an impossible situation by rejecting him. Though Saul is imperfect, nothing in the story suggests that he is deserving of such torture and suffering. Though the answer to this riddle, like that of love and God's preferences and plans, ultimately is unsolvable, I suspect that God's behavior might stem from God's own victimization. That

25. As I noted in the first chapter, love is used in covenants to describe the binding relationship between the treaty partners. In these treaties, both partners, whether unequal or not, are expected to love—that is, to be loyal to the covenant and provide service—to the other (William Moran, "The Ancient Near Eastern Background of the Love of God in Deuteronomy," *CBQ* 25, no. 1[1963]: 79). Considering these connotations, the lack of mention of David's love of Saul suggests David's lack of loyalty to Saul. That is, Saul, in loving David, appears to give David something akin to loyalty and service. Saul, however, does not receive the same expected loyalty and service from David in return. As such, this statement about Saul's love at 1 Samuel 16:21 hints of Saul's misjudgment and underestimation of David's loyalties and ambitions, and in so doing, foreshadows the coming political machinations and seizure of Saul's throne by David.

26. Indeed, David will ultimately prove iatrogenic or a kind of pharmakon—that is, both the poison and the curse.

is, God, in his harsh treatment of Saul, behaves like someone who has just experienced his own heartbreak.

Who is this beloved who might have spurned God's love? Both the immediate literary context of the story as well as other more "distant" biblical texts suggest a possible answer. Turning first to the "neighborhood" of the tale, the triple stories of Saul's enthronement is preceded by a revealing argument, which ends with something that looks a lot like divine heartbreak. First Samuel 8 recounts how the elders of Israel, after declaring Samuel's sons unsuitable as successors for the prophet, demand that Samuel appoint a king for Israel. When Samuel relays this request to God, God responds with something approaching forlornness: "and the LORD said to Samuel, 'Listen to the voice of the people in all that they say to you, for they have not rejected you, but they have rejected me from being king over them'" (1 Sam. 8:7). Whether logical or not, according to God, the people's request for a king is tantamount to a rejection of God. For God, it signifies an act of divine replacement and signals a desire by Israel to either "breakup" with God or at least make their relationship less exclusive.[27]

Looking at the stories that follow, it is not difficult to read in Saul's selection the actions of an angry and dejected deity. In reaction to rejection and heartbreak, God reluctantly chooses a king, but as this human king is the first to replace God the king, God deliberately chooses someone with shortcomings, someone unlikely to succeed, and, as it comes to be, someone temporary. To use modern parlance, Saul appears to be a rebound—for both God and Israel, or more accurately, a rebound that God passive-aggressively chooses for Israel. By choosing someone of lesser permanence and ability, God can prove both to himself and to Israel that a human king was indeed a mistake. Moreover, the people can also be punished for their request by experiencing firsthand the repercussions of their folly. And indeed, there are both immediate and far-reaching repercussions to kingship. In the immediate aftermath, David and Saul's battle for the throne leads to death and a civil war, while later in the text, kingship will be blamed for Israel's heresy and, ultimately, its destruction (2 Kgs. 21:11–13).

Other biblical texts also support the idea that divine heartbreak might be behind God's unkind behavior toward Saul. Again, we find that—though God is said to love other things, such as righteousness (Pss. 11:7; 33:5), justice (Ps. 37:28; Isa. 61:8), haters of evil (Ps. 97:10), and the temple (Mal. 2:11)—God's main love in the Hebrew text is Israel (Deut. 4:37, 7:13, 10:15; 2 Chr. 20:7; Pss. 47:4, 78:68; Isa. 41:8; 43:4; 48:14; Jer. 30:14; Hos. 11:1, 14:4; Mal. 1:2). That is, according to the Hebrew Scriptures, it is Israel who is God's soulmate.

27. I am ignoring issues of dating and redaction in my discussion of 1 Samuel 8.

In such a case, it is not at all surprising that God would react rather badly to the people's demand for a king. If this request, according to God, entails a personal rejection by Israel, the "apple of his eye" (Deut. 32:10), God's unfair treatment of Saul, though not justified, becomes comprehensible as the lashing out of unrequited love. The account of Saul—his selection and rejection by God, and his love of and betrayal by David at the bidding of God—therefore might entail an elongated biblical rendering of the much-repeated aphorism "hurt people hurt people."[28]

God's heartbreak might also explain—though again not justify—why Saul himself is the first to come to love David, his usurper. Saul, in trusting, being vulnerable to, feeling a kinship toward, and being the first to love David, relives or mimics God's situation vis-à-vis Israel. That is, God undoubtedly trusts, is vulnerable to, feels an affinity for, and is the first character to love Israel. Both Saul and God, moreover, are also cruelly hurt and betrayed by their beloveds. Considering that Saul's pain, in so far as it is caused by a bad spirit, is mainly spiritual or metaphysical, and considering that it comes on the heels of an argument and rejection, it is not too far to think that Saul's suffering broadly overlaps with that of God. Indeed, Saul has always been described as particularly susceptible to spiritual influences (1 Sam. 10:9–13, 18:10, 19:18–24). As such, it is plausible that Saul picks up on and replays God's own suffering and heartbreak. Hence, whether out of malice, heartbreak, or maybe even simply a desire for empathy, Israel's first king, God, seems to have put Israel's first *human* king, Saul, quite literally in his place: the new monarch experiences the same rejection by his beloved that the old monarch, God, experienced.

CONCLUSION

The tale of Saul and David is a theologically troubling story and makes our understanding of love more problematic and complex. Centered on God's mysterious appointment and equally mysterious rejection of Saul as king, this chapter outlined the cruel twist of fate or, more accurately, divine planning, that eventually leads to the downfall of the divinely rejected Saul and the ascent of God's newly favored, David. Of central interest are the ways in which God uses love as a powerful tool to make Saul vulnerable to a power-hungry usurper. That Saul falls victim to love and comes to love his own usurper adds to the tragic portrayal. As such, not only does the story of David

28. Matthew Phelan, "The History of 'Hurt People Hurt People,'" *Slate*, September 17, 2019, https://slate.com/culture/2019/09/hurt-people-hurt-people-quote-origin-hustlers-phrase .html.

and Saul evince a dark vision of love, but it also brings out the tragedy of Saul, the victim of both God and of love.

As with the story of Esau and Jacob, the empathic portrayal of Saul and, by extension, the possibly empathetic portrayal of God complicates out reading of love. As I proposed, God might not just be a victimizer of love, but might also be its victim. Rejected by his beloved, Israel, as its sole king, a grief-stricken and brokenhearted God lashes out: God, the first divine king of Israel, forces Saul, the first human king of Israel, to experience the same sort of love, rejection, and heartbreak that God himself experienced. Through this mimicry, the narrative shows that, when it comes to love, the line between human characters and God overlaps to a surprising degree. Love and heartbreak are things shared by God and by human characters alike. While the story of Jacob and Esau compared two "kinds" of loves and asserted the superiority and divinity of true love, the story of Saul and David goes further: It posits that, like humans, God too is vulnerable to love and its effects. In so doing, the story portrays love as a source of great power, a power equal to or perhaps even greater than God. Love, this story begins to suggest, might itself be a divine force of overwhelming and indescribable magnitude.

4

The Pain and Mystery of Love

Jonathan and David

INTRODUCTION

The relationship between Jonathan, the firstborn son of Saul, and David has long fascinated interpreters. Filled with tales of secret alliances and meetings, dysfunctional families, and a struggle for the throne, the operatic drama of these two "lovers" (1 Sam. 18–20, 31; 2 Sam. 1) is capped off by the tragic death of Jonathan, slain in battle—a death that is mourned by the remaining party in a moving lament: "I am distressed for you, my brother Jonathan; greatly beloved were you to me; your love to me was wonderful, passing the love of women" (2 Sam. 1:26). The repeated use of love in the stories about these characters in 1 Samuel (1 Sam. 18:1, 3; 20:17) cannot but remind readers of other star-crossed lovers, such as Romeo and Juliet or, more fittingly, Achilles and Patroclus. Understandably, readers have wondered about the nature of Jonathan and David's relationship and whether they were a same-sex couple.

As we have seen, however, when it comes to love things are not so simple. Rather, as I have tried to show, love (*ahav*) in the Hebrew text is dense and ambiguous, capable of affecting characters in both delightful and devastating ways. In particular, this chapter focuses on the complicated love triangle between Jonathan, David, and Saul, and shows how God's rejection of Saul ultimately taints their love relationships. As I explained in the previous chapter, God suddenly and mysteriously switches his favor from Saul to David without an apparent reason. This divine betrayal contaminates the relationship between Saul and those closest to him, especially his son Jonathan,

71

leading to division, pain, and more betrayal. Not only will father and son wind up turning on each other, but as the consequences of divine rejection spread, so they will be betrayed by the one character whom they both love: David. David, in turn, with the help of God, will use the escalating fracturing of Saul's family to rise to power, obtain love, and ultimately seize Saul's throne—the throne that was meant for Jonathan. In so doing, the story of Jonathan and David shows the immense power of love to cause havoc, suffering, pain, and, ultimately, death.

JONATHAN, THE DIVINELY FAVORED

We first meet Jonathan whose name means "YHWH has given" or "gift of YHWH"—a fitting name, as I will discuss—at 1 Samuel 13:2, immediately after the account of his father's anointment as king. Pious, militarily skilled, and astute, Jonathan bears the hallmarks of a hero from the very beginning. Introduced without much fanfare at 1 Samuel 13:2, he is said to be put in charge of one-third of his father's troops. Saul's confidence is well-founded: Jonathan, in the very next verse (13:3), immediately defeats a garrison of the Philistines, Israel's enemy. Considering that military abilities are an essential feature of successful ancient Near Eastern kings, this description of the immediate military success of Jonathan speaks to his future potential as a successful monarch.[1]

Yet embedded in the good news are signs of coming trouble. Already a sense of contrast can be detected between father and son, foreshadowing tensions between them. The more emphasis there is on Jonathan's military abilities, the more Saul's abilities appear deficient in comparison. Indeed, while Jonathan's successes in battle are noted in 1 Samuel 13, there is no such note of Saul's military achievements. With only one-third of the troops, Jonathan manages to do what his father, the king, fails to do with double the number (13:2). Worse still, Saul claims Jonathan's victory as his own: "When all of Israel heard that *Saul* had defeated the garrison of the Philistines . . ." (1 Sam. 13:4; emphasis added). Though father and son are fighting on the same side, the confusion over Saul and Jonathan is telling. It appears that it is Jonathan, not Saul, who is the more militarily talented of the two, and if so, uncomfortable questions are raised as to why Saul remains king and whether it is time for him to move aside for his promising heir.

---

1. Cynthia R. Chapman, *The Gendered Language of Warfare in the Israelite-Assyrian Encounter,* HSM 62 (Winona Lake: Eisenbrauns, 2004), esp. 20–59, 83.

Saul's first rejection by God shortly after Jonathan's victory confirms these doubts (1 Sam. 13). As I discussed in the previous chapter, God mysteriously rejects Saul as king twice, once in 1 Samuel 13 and again in 1 Samuel 15, both times for what appear to be minor deficiencies in communication. Tellingly, during the first rejection, God tells Saul through the prophet Samuel that God will now seek a man "after his own heart" to be appointed ruler in Saul's stead (vv. 13–14). Considering that Jonathan's military successes are described right before the first rejection and considering that Jonathan is Saul's firstborn heir, it is natural to assume that Jonathan is the man-after-God's-own-heart who will come to succeed and replace Saul.

God's message to Saul during his first rejection is ambiguous on this matter. God states that Saul's rule will no longer be established forever but that it will come to an end (1 Sam. 13:13–14). The meaning of "Saul's rule" and "forever" are unclear, however.[2] Does God mean Saul specifically or rather the House of Saul, which would, of course, include Jonathan? David, who takes over for Saul, does eventually become part of Saul's family as he marries Saul's daughter Michal (1 Sam. 18:27). Moreover, what is meant by "forever"? Does it mean that Saul's dynasty will come to an end immediately or eventually? God's deliberately unclear message to Saul leaves room for interpretation and therefore enough wiggle room for Jonathan to be viewed as a possible replacement for Saul or, at least, for Saul to think of Jonathan as such.

The chapter that follows the first rejection of Saul, which describes another military victory by Jonathan—this time single-handedly (1 Sam. 14:1–15)—even more strongly suggests that Jonathan is the "man after his own heart" intended by God to replace Saul (13:14). Bespeaking his piety, Jonathan, before his surprise solo ambush of the Philistines, tells his armor-bearer that, despite appearances, this attack is far from a suicide mission because "the LORD will act for us; for nothing can hinder the LORD from saving by many or by few" (1 Sam. 14:6). The armor-bearer, in turn, replies with a telling statement that references and repeats a key term from God's rejection of Saul in the previous chapter (1 Sam. 13): "Do all that your heart [*levaveka*] inclines. Indeed, I am with you! As your heart [*levaveka*], so is mine"[3] (1 Sam. 14:7; my translation). Considering that in the preceding story Samuel tells Saul that he will be replaced by a man after God's own *heart* (*levavo*) (1 Sam. 13:13–14), the repeated mention of Jonathan's "heart"

---

2. On the ambiguity of Saul's rule, see Michael Avioz, "Could Saul Rule Forever?: A New Look at 1 Samuel 13:13–14," *Journal of Hebrew Scriptures* 5 (2005): n.p.

3. See previous chapter on the various meanings of "heart."

(*levav*) by his armor-bearer echoes God's statement and appears to confirm Jonathan as the successor foretold by Samuel.

Jonathan's replacement of his father as king would also mitigate some of the theological problems caused by God's mysterious rejection of Saul. God first rejects Saul as king at 1 Samuel 13 for what seems to be an inconsequential offense—miscommunication and misinterpretation of Samuel's instruction. If God intends to punish Saul for this mistake by simply replacing him with his own son, the militarily talented and divinely favored crown prince, then the punishment better fits the crime. For a minor offense, Saul receives a minor punishment: early retirement.

God's reaction to Jonathan's successful solo attack suggests that this might be exactly what God (originally) had in mind (1 Sam. 14). During his surprise attack, affirming that Jonathan possesses the twin traits—faithfulness and military prowess—needed to be a good king, God validates Jonathan's statement "that the LORD will act for us" (1 Sam. 14:6) by doing exactly that. That is, God "acts for" Jonathan by causing "a panic in the camp, in the field, and among all the people," trembling, and an earthquake (14:15)—all signs of the presence of YHWH, especially YHWH in the form of a warrior (Exod. 15:12; Josh. 10:10; Judg. 5:4; Isa. 29:6). Not only does Jonathan's faithfulness seem to have persuaded God to join in on the fight, but the natural phenomena put Jonathan in the company of other great Israelite heroes, such as Moses, Joshua, and Elijah, who also experience YHWH in the form of an earthquake, trembling, or panic (Exod. 15:12; Josh. 10:10; 1 Kgs. 19:11).

Every indication therefore appears to confirm that the crown prince, Jonathan—a man who exhibits remarkable faithfulness, bravery, and military skill, a man who is favored by God, his armor-bearer and, as we will soon see, his fellow soldiers—likely is the man-after-God's-own-heart predicted to replace Saul. Yet like the calm before a storm, ominous signs portend a different outcome. The sign, as in the previous stories we have examined, centers on contrast. Despite his superlative portrayal, Jonathan, strangely, is never said to be loved by anyone. This is especially odd when we compare him to David, who is said to be loved by nearly everyone. Divine favoritism and approval, as we saw in the last chapter, should have led to love and therefore loyalty and power, especially political power. Yet no one is said to love Jonathan, not even his own father, Saul, who is only ever said to love one person: David (1 Sam. 16:21). The absence of love, in revealing the contrast between Jonathan and David, foreshadows their contrasting fates. The lack of love, moreover, also speaks to the reason behind Jonathan's failure to live up to his promise: Saul's ambivalence, possibly even fear and jealousy, of his divinely favored and talented son, all of which will not only take Jonathan out of contention as successor but will also leave him dead.

SAUL'S BETRAYAL OF JONATHAN

The sequence of stories in 1 Samuel confirms that Jonathan's military successes and clear favoritism by God are the source of the discord and tension between father and son. Though the order of events is confusing, 1 Samuel 14 describes how during or just prior to Jonathan's triumphant engagement with the Philistines, Saul, unbeknownst to Jonathan, curses everyone from eating before battle (1 Sam. 14:24). This fasting vow is made out of earshot of Jonathan, who subsequently eats a bit of honey, which is said to brighten (*'ur*) Jonathan's eyes (14:27).[4] "To brighten" (*'ur*) sounds a lot like "to curse" (*'rr*) and suggests that Jonathan's unintentional contravention of his father's vow has unleashed a curse.[5] When Saul later asks God whether he should go to battle and hears no reply, he realizes that God's silence is due to the contravention of this vow; and through the use of lots—a kind of sacred dice— Saul discovers that the vow-breaker is his very own son, Jonathan (1 Sam. 14:36–42). Tellingly, lots, which were used earlier to designate Saul as king (1 Sam. 10:20–24), are now used to end Saulide rule by identifying Jonathan as the vow-breaker and, therefore, disqualifying him from the throne. Saul, in short, curses himself.

Saul's reaction to the discovery of the vow-breaker bespeaks his guilt. A vow or a curse in the Hebrew text was serious business. More than mere speech, they were magical, meaningful, and irreversible incantations. Hence, we would expect Saul, as a parent, to be shocked and horrified to discover that the breaker of an irreversible vow is his own son. Yet Saul, after finding out that a family member he loves (or ought to love), indeed, his heir, is now certainly doomed because of a foolish vow he made instead doubles down, swearing to surely kill Jonathan: "Saul said, 'God do so to me and more also; you shall surely die'" (14:44). Instead of trying to prevent Jonathan's death, Saul seems eager for it.

Saul's strange behavior does not stop there. Even before the identification of the vow-breaker, he swears that even if "it is my son Jonathan, he shall surely die!" (14:39). Though this might be an attempt by Saul to appear unquestionably fair, it is fishy that Saul mentions Jonathan's demise just before his son is identified as the guilty party. Saul's unflinching reaction once Jonathan is indeed discovered to be the culprit makes it seem as though the outcome is not entirely undesired.

---

4. On why the verb at 1 Sam. 14:27, 29 should be read as from the root aleph-waw-resh (*'wr*) and not resh-aleph-heh (*r'h*), see A. Graeme Auld, *I & II Samuel: A Commentary* (Louisville: Westminster John Knox, 2011), 157.

5. A. Graeme Auld writes, "In an unvocalized text, the consonants *wt'mh* (v. 27) can be read either 'and they [Jonathan's eyes] shone' or 'and they were cursed'" (*I & II Samuel*, 157).

It is unclear, therefore, whether Saul is foolish or savvy. He is either extremely careless, so careless that he makes a lethal vow without first checking to see if his family members, especially his heir, are present; or he is savvy, setting up his son for failure by deliberately uttering a curse while Jonathan is absent or out of earshot. Considering Saul's odd reaction, and considering that Saul is not the first parent to try to murder their child in the Hebrew Bible (Gen. 22; Judg. 11:29–40; 2 Kgs. 3:27), his behavior nudges the reader to the more alarming reading—that Saul suspected or knew that the guilty party would be his son and deliberately uttered a curse that would damn him.

Why would Saul do such an insane thing? Though the biblical text does not tells us of Saul's motivations, a careful reading suggests a possible cause: Saul is jealous and fearful that Jonathan is indeed the "man after God's own heart" whom Samuel predicted will replace him as king (1 Sam. 13).[6] Not wanting to go down alone or perhaps terrified that Jonathan might make the first move to remove him from the throne, something which David's son Absalom will try to do to his dear old dad later in the stories (2 Sam. 15), Saul deliberately makes a vow without checking to see if everyone, especially his promising heir, is in attendance. Perceiving his son as a political rival, Saul therefore attempts to quash Jonathan before he becomes a bigger threat.

Perhaps Saul's suspicions are not entirely misplaced. Indeed, not just Saul, but Jonathan too might have started to identify his father as a possible political rival. When Jonathan eats honey and is told of his father's vow, he calls it an '*akar*—usually translated as "trouble" (1 Sam. 14:29)—and criticizes it as a foolish *military* move (14:29–30). Considering that guiding and overseeing the military was one of the main duties of a king, Jonathan's criticism of his father's vow expresses doubts over Saul's ability to lead and therefore to rule. Moreover, Jonathan's criticism comes immediately after Saul's first rejection by God as king. The timing is suggestive and hints of Jonathan's knowledge of the rejection and also possibly his agreement with it. Perhaps Jonathan also has doubts, maybe longstanding, about Saul's leadership; and after God's rejection, perhaps he has been itching to take over. After all, God has already stated that his father's days on the throne were numbered. Who better to take the reins of the reign than Saul's firstborn son, the rightful heir?

The use of '*akar* in other places in the Hebrew Bible clearly reveals that Saul's vow and Jonathan's reaction to it concern power, politics, and rivalry. The term '*akar* is used in Judges 11 to describe the foolish and rash vow made by Jephthah, a military hero and judge, that he would sacrifice whatever greets him first when he successfully returns from battle, which just happens to be his unnamed, virgin daughter (Judg. 11:35). Considering that Jephthah's vow stems from his desire

---

6. Auld, *I & II Samuel*, 156.

to win a battle so that he can be reinstated into a community that has rejected him and also become its political leader or "head" (Judg. 11:9), the use of *'akar* to describe both Jephthah's and Saul's vows suggests that, as with Jephthah, Saul's vow also has something to do with political power.

As such, it is not difficult to speculate about Saul's possible motivations for the vow and curse. Perhaps Saul believes that eliminating Jonathan as his rival would help him expiate his mistake and undo God's rejection. Perhaps like Jephthah, Saul too envisions Jonathan as a potential sacrifice, a worthy exchange for the continuation of power. After all, 2 Kings 3 describes a great divine wrath that is unleashed after the sacrifice of the crown prince of Moab by his father, the king, showing that the sacrifice of firstborn children, especially royal, firstborn males, had tremendous political, military, and divine power.

If this was Saul's plan, he fails. The other soldiers refuse to let the crown prince be killed after Jonathan's earlier victory over the Philistines and force Saul to renege on his word (1 Sam. 14:45). Jonathan's popularity with the troops and his military talent, in compelling Saul to relent, lends further credence to the idea that Saul was motivated by jealousy and fear when he made the vow. As the intervention shows, it is his son, not Saul, whom the soldiers respect and obey. More importantly, if Saul's vow comes from his fear of losing power, it has the opposite effect: it—specifically, the soldiers' temporary blockage of the vow's fulfillment—affirms that Saul's fall from power is certain and indeed nigh. Considering that the first rejection by God stemmed in part from Saul's attempt to placate his impatient troops from abandoning the battlefield by offering a sacrifice before Samuel's arrival (1 Sam. 13: 8–12), Saul's inability to stand up to the troops in order to fulfill an irreversible vow, albeit an unnecessary one, shows that Saul lacks the control and authority befitting his station. Considering that to fail as general is to fail as king, it is safe to say that Saul's days are assuredly numbered.

What Saul does accomplish with his vow is to ensure that Jonathan will go down with him. Saul ends up contaminating his son with the effects of the divine rejection that he so desperately wants to escape. Despite the soldiers' (and God's) obvious preference for Jonathan, Saul's vow effectively takes his son out of contention as his successor, as the vow and its curse, though paused, cannot be undone. Saul and Jonathan's family history confirms the inevitability of the fulfillment of this vow and curse. Rachel, the famous ancestress of the tribe of Benjamin of which Saul and Jonathan are members, similarly falls victim to a lethal vow made by a family member (Gen. 31). Jonathan and Saul therefore appear to be destined to follow in her footsteps and reenact this earlier family tragedy.[7]

---

7. Rachel steals her father's teraphim (Gen. 31:19), which are sacred objects that are humanoid in shape, the function and meaning of which are heavily debated by scholars. Later,

The impending doom of Jonathan and Saul reveals the potency and power of love to cause pain and suffering. As I discussed in the previous chapter, Saul gets on the wrong side of a deity for reasons that might have to do with God's own heartbreak. Saul's betrayal of Jonathan therefore is part of the unfolding consequences of divine rejection—a rejection that is envisioned as a kind of contagion. As such, Saul's rejection by God leads to a decrease in political power, love, loyalty, and regard—not just for him but also for everyone associated with him. Especially affected are Saul's kin, who see a sudden and shocking loss of status and even come to turn on each other.[8] Hence, like an invisible but disastrous fracture, divine rejection and the loss of love that follows plunges Saul, his immediate family, his clan, his tribe, and his nation into collapse and ruin as they all turn against each other. The schisms and betrayals in the family—between God and Saul, Samuel and Saul, and now Jonathan and Saul—provide the perfect opportunity for God's newly chosen favorite, David, to sneak into Saul's house and snatch the throne right from under Saul's nose.

---

when Rachel's father shows up and searches for them, her husband, Jacob, not knowing of the theft, vows that whoever stole the teraphim shall not live (Gen. 31:32). Tragically, this vow is fulfilled when Rachel dies while giving birth to Benjamin, the very ancestor for whom Saul's tribe is named. Though her death during labor initially seems unrelated to her theft, parallel images reveal the connection. Rachel hides the teraphim from her father by sitting on it and claiming that she is menstruating (Gen. 31:35). Her concealment of the teraphim in so far as it entails blood and squatting on a small, humanoid figure mimics childbirth, and hints that her death during labor was the result of her theft and the vow that came from it (W. G. Plath and W. H. Hollow, *The Torah: A Modern Commentary* [New York: Union for Reform Judaism, 1981], 214). More importantly, this allusion and connection to his ancestress Rachel signals that Jonathan will undoubtedly follow in her footsteps and also fall victim to a lethal vow made by a family member. On teraphims, see Karel van der Toorn, "The Nature of the Biblical Teraphim in the Light of Cuneiform Evidence," *Catholic Biblical Quarterly* 52 (1990): 203–4. Rachel's motivations are debated: Cyrus H. Gordon, "The Story of Jacob and Laban in the Light of the Nuzi Tablets," *Bulletin of the American Schools of Oriental Research* 66 (1937): 25–27; M. Heltzer, "New Light from Emar on Genesis 31: The Theft of the Teraphim," in *"Und Mose schrieb dieses Lied auf": Studien zum Alten Testament und zum Alten Orient. Festschrift für Oswald Loretz zur Vollendung seines 70*, ed. M. Dietrich and I. Kottsieper (Münster: Ugarit-Verlag, 1998), 357–62; Anne-Marie Korte, "Significance Obscured: Rachel's Theft of the Teraphim: Divinity and Corporeality in Gen. 31," in *Begin with the Body: Corporeality, Religion and Gender*, ed. Jonneke Bekkenkamp and Maaike de Haardt (Leuven: Peeters, 1998), 157–82; Theodore J. Lewis, "The Ancestral Estate (*naḥalat 'elohim*) in 2 Samuel 14:16," *Journal of Biblical Literature* 110, no. 4 (1991): 597–612; H. Rouillard and J. Tropper, "*Trpym*, rituels de guérison et culte des ancêtres d'après 1 Samuel XIX 11–17 et les textes parallèles d'Assur et de Nuzi," *Vetus Testamentum* 37, fasc. 3 (1987): 351–57; E. A. Speiscr, *Genesis* (Garden City, NY: Doubleday, 1962), 250.

8. That it is the family that is the most affected by divine preference is understandable when we consider that the Hebrew text is a product of and therefore reflects the kin and family-based structure of the ancient Near East.

JONATHAN AND DAVID'S RELATIONSHIP

The darker side of love, including betrayal, death, and dynastic collapse reaches its climax when Jonathan meets and befriends David. First Samuel 18 describes their intense introduction:

> When David had finished speaking to Saul, the soul [*nephesh*] of Jonathan was bound to the soul [*nephesh*] of David, and Jonathan loved [*ahav*] him as his own soul [*nephesh*]. Saul took him that day and would not let him return to his father's house. Then Jonathan made a covenant with David because he loved [*ahav*] him as his own soul [*nephesh*]. (1 Sam. 18:1–3)

Like Saul who comes to love David quickly after their meeting, so also Jonathan falls victim to David's charms and is immediately and repeatedly said to love David (1 Sam. 18:1, 3). This love, moreover, is so contagious that Saul and Jonathan's love will quickly be followed by that of Michal, Jonathan's sister and Saul's daughter, the court, and the people of Israel (1 Sam. 18:16, 20, 22, 28).

Considering the charged introduction, interpreters have long wondered whether the story of David and Jonathan describes a same-sex relationship and whether these characters were gay or bisexual. Undoubtedly, this has led to an immense amount of scholarship. For the sake of our analysis of love, I will quickly summarize the various positions on this question, which largely fall within an interpretive spectrum.[9]

On the one end are those who view the tale of David and Jonathan as clearly indicative of a same-sex relationship.[10] Nancy Wilson, for example, describes David as "the most clearly bisexual figure in the whole of the Bible," and that Jonathan is "more truly gay" than David.[11] Similarly, Theodore Jennings states that the introduction of Jonathan and David should be considered as "love at first sight," and that, not just Jonathan, but Saul, too, had a sexual

---

9. Erin E. Fleming, "Political Favoritism in Saul's Court: נעם, חפץ, and the Relationship between David and Jonathan," *Journal of Biblical Literature* 135, no. 1 (2016): 19–34.

10. John Boswell, *Christianity, Social Tolerance, and Homosexuality: Gay People in Western Europe from the Beginning of the Christian Era to the Fourteenth Century* (Chicago: University of Chicago Press, 1980); John Boswell, *Same-Sex Unions in Premodern Europe* (New York: Vintage, 1994), esp. 136–37, 182; Jody Hirsh, "In Search of Role Models," in *Twice Blessed: On Being Lesbian, Gay, and Jewish*, ed. Christie Balka and Andy Rose (Boston: Beacon, 1989), 83–91; Thomas M. Horner, *Jonathan Loved David: Homosexuality in Biblical Times* (Philadelphia: Westminster, 1978); Theodore W. Jennings Jr., *Jacob's Wound: Homoerotic Narratives in the Literature of Ancient Israel* (New York: Continuum, 2005).

11. Nancy Wilson, *Our Tribe: Queer Folks, God, Jesus, and the Bible* (San Francisco: HarperSanFrancisco, 1995), 149, 151.

relationship with David.[12] These overlapping sexual relationships are, according to Jennings, the basis of the conflict among the three.[13]

In the middle are those commentators who are less sure about how to classify David and Jonathan's relationship.[14] Noting that being gay and its meanings reflect contemporary understandings and designations of sexual identity, which differ from those in the ancient Near East, these scholars argue that the story of Jonathan and David's relationship should be, at best, viewed as evincing homoerotic allusions, images, and terminology, many of which are comparable to similar images or ideas found in other ancient Near Eastern myths, such as the famous ancient Mesopotamian tale known as the Epic of Gilgamesh.[15] Many of these commentators note that the story of David and Jonathan arises from the homosocial culture of the ancient Near East and ancient Israel, and therefore reflects the social, political, theological, and gender significance of male social bonds and connections.[16]

On the other end of the interpretative spectrum are those who view Jonathan and David's story as largely devoid of homoerotic or same-sex meanings, terminology, or imagery. Instead, using William Moran's influential article on love in Deuteronomy, these interpreters argue that love (*ahav*) in the stories about Jonathan and David, like in Deuteronomy, has a largely political or

---

12. Jennings, *Jacob's Wound*, 25.

13. Jennings, *Jacob's Wound*, 17–25.

14. Silvia Schroer and Thomas Staubli second this idea that the "passion" between David and Jonathan might be connected to Saul's growing jealousy of David. They demure, however, on definitively asserting that this relationship was gay, arguing instead that "David and Jonathan shared a homoerotic and, more than likely, a homosexual relationship" ("Saul, David and Jonathan—The Story of a Triangle? A Contribution to the Issue of Homosexuality in the First Testament," in *A Feminist Companion to Samuel and Kings*, ed. Athalya Brenner [Sheffield: Sheffield Academic, 2000], 22–36).

15. Anthony Heacock, "Wrongly Framed? The 'David and Jonathan Narrative' and the Writing of Biblical Homosexuality," *The Bible and Critical Theory* 3, no. 2 (2007): 1–22; David Nolan Fewell and David M. Gunn, *Gender, Power, and Promise: The Subject of the Bible's First Story* (Nashville: Abingdon, 1993); Martti Nissinen, *Homoeroticism in the Biblical World* (Minneapolis: Fortress, 1998); Martti Nissinen, "Die Liebe von David und Jonatan als Frage der modernen Exegese," *Biblica* 80, no. 2 (1999): 250–63; Thomas Römer and Loyse Bonjour, *L'homosexualité dans le Proche-Orient ancien et la Bible* (Genève: Labor et Fides, 2005), esp. 61–102; Susan Ackerman, *When Heroes Love: The Ambiguity of Eros in the Stories of Gilgamesh and David* (New York: Columbia University Press, 2005).

16. Nissinen, *Homoeroticism in the Biblical World*, 128. Nissinen also maintains that this story attests to the presence of an "inter-male culture" ("zwischenmännlicher Kultur") where love among men ("Männerliebe"), one which excludes women, was seen as "more wonderful" ("wunderbarer") than love for women (Nissinen, "Die Liebe," 259). So also Jennings notes that this story "is set within a context of a warrior society, which takes for granted that male heroes are accompanied by younger or lower-status males," a context which, as a result, is open to "same-sex erotic attachment and practice" (Jennings, *Jacob's Wound*, xiii).

covenantal, not erotic, meaning.[17] As evidence, they note that, outside Song of Songs, *ahav* is mainly used to talk about the relationship between YHWH and Israel, that is, in a covenantal sense, only sometimes used to talk about "intimate interpersonal relationships" ("intime zwischenmenschliche Beziehung"), and never to describe a same-sex relationship ("homosexuelle Beziehung").[18] Indeed, so persuasive is this argument that even commentators who note the erotic or homosocial features of Jonathan and David's tale also acknowledge that the story has an undeniable political purpose—to justify David's usurpation of Saul's throne.[19]

When the biblical story of Jonathan and David is considered in the original Hebrew, it is easy to see why there is such a broad range of interpretations. Not only does their story use *ahav*, love, multiple times, but the writers or editors add to the confusion and ambiguity of Jonathan and David's relationship by also using another dense term alongside it, *nephesh*, which is usually translated as "soul" (1 Sam. 18:1, 3; 20:17). The term *nephesh*, which is found 754 times in the Hebrew Bible, refers to animals and people, both to their affections, appetites, mind, will, activity, as well as their inner living component. Meaning "throat," *nephesh* can by extension "become the symbol of the needy, greedy human being, of the élan vital, the power that makes the human being the creature that pants for and craves life."[20]

Though I will discuss *ahav* and *nephesh* in more detail shortly, what is immediately evident is that the narrative, through the use of two dense terms,

17. On love in Deuteronomy, see William Moran, "The Ancient Near Eastern Background of the Love of God in Deuteronomy," *Catholic Biblical Quarterly* 25, no. 1 (1963).

18. Markus Zehnder, "Exegetische Beobachtungen zu den David-Jonathan-Geschichten," *Biblica* 79, no. 2 (1998): 155. The other reasons Zehnder names are (1) the literary context of these stories describes David's rise to become king, and therefore has a political purpose—namely, to show Jonathan's recognition, facilitation, and support of David's takeover of the throne; (2) the forbidding of sexual relations between men in Lev. 18:22 and 20:13; (3) the centrality of David in later messianism, which Zehnder maintains would have been unlikely if interpreters viewed him as part of a same-sex relationship; and (4) the description of David and Jonathan as having wives and children, that is, as participating in heterosexual relationships (Zehnder, "Exegetische Beobachtungen," 173–76).

19. Ackerman, *When Heroes Love*, 227–28. Though interpretations vary, Saul Olyan well encapsulates the general position of many biblical scholars when he writes that "it is not at all clear that the tenth-century BCE apologists responsible for the 'History of David's Rise' would have been particularly bothered by a homoerotic meaning of the love comparison of 2 Sam. 1:26. What is clear, however, is that a central priority of the apologists . . . is to show that David was innocent of the deaths of Saul, Jonathan, Abner, Eshbaal, and other Saulides who stood in the way of his ascent to the throne" ("'Surpassing the Love of Women': Another Look at 2 Samuel 1:26 and the Relationship of David and Jonathan," in *Authorizing Marriage? Canon, Tradition, and Critique in the Blessing of Same-Sex Unions*, ed. Mark D. Jordan [Princeton: Princeton University Press, 2006], 7–16 [15]).

20. Thomas Staubli and Silvia Schroer, *Body Symbolism in the Bible*, trans. Linda M. Maloney (Collegeville: Liturgical Press, 2001), 56–67 (57).

shrouds David and Jonathan's relationship in mystery. Indeed, considering it is oftentimes hard to decipher the boundaries between the different types of love in life outside of the text—the movement from friendship to "something more," for example—how much more difficult, if not impossible, is it to assess, categorize, and understand the significance and type of love relationships between characters in an ancient tale? This is especially the case as love, both in life and as reflected in the biblical text, does not have one solid meaning but consists of a messy, overlapping assortment of meanings and associations.

Some of the confusion, however, is intentional. That is, I think that the writer or editors deliberately use *ahav* and *nephesh* in association with David precisely because they are dense and multivalent, and therefore apt terms through which to hint and suggest but never fully and clearly reveal. And the writers or editors had good reasons to obscure David's story, especially that of his rise to power. Considering that David's story culminates with the deaths of Saul and his heirs, and his takeover of Saul's throne, such a tale undoubtedly necessitated a narrative (and terms) that blurs and blinkers, that hides and conceals.[21]

In particular, the use of these terms adds to and heightens the ambiguity and confusion of David's relationships, especially the one with the crown prince, Jonathan. And in so doing, their relationship comes off as much more personal and intimate—and therefore difficult to comprehend for anyone outside of it. Moreover, the use of these terms, by hiking up the personal and intimate feel of the narrative, adds to the emotional weight of their story, and therefore transforms it and the relationship described in it into something more tragic, more fated—something almost mythic: star-crossed, as it were. As a result, as myth, the nature of their relationship becomes even more difficult to ascertain, and, therefore alongside it, David's true motivations and feelings. The density, intimacy, and fated feel all work to utterly and wholly conceal David, making him unapproachable and impenetrable. Like love, David, whose name fittingly means "beloved," therefore becomes largely invisible, only discernible through the text darkly and in glimpses.

JONATHAN AND DAVID AS DOUBLES

Despite the difficulty, what is clear—especially when we consider the contours of Jonathan and David's story—is that their love relationship centers on

21. Baruch Halpern, *David's Secret Demons: Messiah, Murderer, Traitor, King* (Grand Rapids: Eerdmans, 2001); P. Kyle McCarter, "The Apology of David," *Journal of Biblical Literature* 99, no. 4 (1980): 489–504; P. Kyle McCarter, "The Historical David," *Interpretation* 40, no. 2 (1986): 117–29; Keith Whitelam, "The Defence of David," *Journal for the Study of the Old Testament* 29 (1984): 61–87.

betrayal, one in a series of betrayals begun by God through God's rejection of Saul. The peculiar portrayal of David and Jonathan as doubles or twins—a portrayal that accentuates Saul's growing separation and loneliness after his rejection by God—highlights the various betrayals that will characterize the interwoven relationships of Saul, David, and Jonathan.

Two accounts of David's entrance into Saul's court elucidate the similarities between David and Jonathan. In one account, David, as a musician, comes to serve Saul when a servant recommends David as "a man of valor, a warrior, prudent in speech, and a man of good presence; and the LORD is with him" (1 Sam. 16:18). As I noted in the preceding chapter, this description goes beyond the qualifications of a mere music therapist and instead emphasizes David's military skill ("man of valor" and "good warrior"), divinely favored status ("skillful in playing [music]" and "the LORD is with him"), and political astuteness ("prudent in speech")—all qualities of a successful king.[22] Interestingly, as we will see, Jonathan is also depicted as gifted with the same abilities.

The second story of David's entrance into Saul's court, the famous tale of David and Goliath (1 Sam. 17), further expands on the servant's description: David, the shepherding, youngest son of Jesse, while delivering lunch to his older brothers who are on the battlefield, overhears Goliath, a Philistine champion of a noted stature, taunting the Israelites and their God. Outraged by what he hears, David bravely and piously volunteers before Saul to fight Goliath.[23] On the battlefield, instead of engaging in hand-to-hand combat with Goliath, David, in an unsubtle dig at Saul, uses a simple sling—a skill that is particularly associated with Saul's tribe, Benjamin (Judg. 20:16)—to successfully kill Goliath (1 Sam. 17:40–50).[24]

This second account again stresses the particular kingly traits of David that were mentioned in the first account: his military skills, piety, divine favoritism, and probably also political astuteness as David, though seemingly a mere shepherd boy, is able to persuade King Saul to allow him to battle a much larger Philistine hero (1 Sam. 17:31–37). As with Jonathan earlier, this description of David as brave, young, pious, and wise contrasts him to Saul who is depicted as cowardly, old, impious, and unwise in comparison. And as with Jonathan, so again with David, it is unclear why Saul remains king when younger, more talented, more pious, and more competent candidates remain in the wings.

22. Steven L. McKenzie, *King David: A Biography* (New York: Oxford University Press, 2000), 51–66.

23. Despite being hired as the music therapist in the preceding chapter, Saul does not appear to recognize David.

24. Suzie Park, "Left-Handed Benjaminites and the Shadow of Saul," *Journal of Biblical Literature* 134, no. 4 (2015): 701–20. Tellingly, 2 Samuel 21:19 states someone else—not David—killed Goliath. On these features of the David and Goliath story, see McKenzie, *King David*, 69–88.

Even more important, these attributes parallel David and Jonathan. As I discussed earlier, Jonathan is also described as a talented and successful military leader (1 Sam. 13:2–4; 14:6–23) whose bravery, like that of David, is matched by and emerges from his piety (1 Sam. 14:6). Moreover, as with David, Jonathan's piety is rewarded by God who guides Jonathan's hand in victory (14:15). David's victory where he impetuously, piously, and fearlessly agrees to fight the Philistine champion, Goliath, only to emerge triumphant with God's help (1 Sam. 17), replays Jonathan's earlier victory where the crown prince undertakes an impetuous, pious, and fearless solo mission against the Philistines, only to emerge triumphant with God's help (1 Sam. 14).

Adding to the similarities, both Jonathan and David are also portrayed as politically savvy and favored by important political factions, such as the military (1 Sam. 18:30). David is described as "prudent in speech" and as having the presence of the Lord ("the LORD is with him") (1 Sam. 16:18). David also possesses enough "shrewdness and intelligence as well as . . . facility with words"[25] to gain entrance into the royal court and attract the attention of the king, the crown prince, and the courtiers. David's political savvy mimics that of Jonathan. In Jonathan's case, he astutely describes Saul's vow of fasting as ʿakar, or troublesome, stating that it is detrimental to the well-being and morale of the soldiers and Israel's overall military success (1 Sam. 14:29–30). This criticism proves correct when Saul's famished soldiers inappropriately start consuming banned animal blood (1 Sam. 14:32). Considering Jonathan's military knowhow and prowess, it is not a surprise that his fellow soldiers prevent him from being murdered by Saul (1 Sam. 14:45). The military undoubtedly are shown to prefer Jonathan—and later David—over Saul.

Both Jonathan and David are therefore depicted as possessing the same regal skill set—military talent, cleverness, piety, divine favoritism, and political astuteness.[26] In contrast, Saul is shown wanting. As a general, he takes a back seat to victories spearheaded by Jonathan and then later David (1 Sam. 18). Moreover, as shown by the fasting vow and its aftermath, he lacks prudence on the battlefield, has difficulty asserting his authority over his soldiers, and is depicted as foolish in speech and thought. Indeed, so inept is Saul that the musician he acquires to help with this affliction—David—the first and only person whom Saul is said to love, turns out to be the very same person who has been secretly anointed king in his stead (1 Sam. 16:1–13). When a real threat to his position comes along, Saul fails to recognize it and is even supportive of it. Saul's mental and spiritual decline is mirrored by his social

25. McKenzie, *King David*, 60. He writes further, "David's 'cleverness of speech' hints at his personal charm and political savvy" (*King David*, 62).

26. Chapman, *Gendered Language*, 20–59, 83; McKenzie, *King David*, 51–66.

decline as political allies and supporters who once gave him wise political advice, such as Samuel, Jonathan, his courtiers, his soldiers, and indeed God himself, all increasingly distance themselves from his side, eventually betraying him for David.

This loss of Saul's faculties cannot be blamed wholly on Saul, however. Rather, as I argued, it is the direct result of God's rejection. Saul, the divinely rejected, serves as a key counterpoint to the doubles, David and Jonathan. Through this comparison, the narrative details the unfortunate consequences of divine rejection and sets the context for the betrayal of Saul by Jonathan, his firstborn son, who aligns with David, the only person whom Saul is ever said to love (1 Sam. 16:21).

JONATHAN'S BETRAYAL OF SAUL AND LOVE OF DAVID

Though Jonathan and David are portrayed as doubles, one key aspect separates them: while Saul is said to love David (1 Sam. 16:21), Saul is never said to love Jonathan. This love, or the lack thereof, in turn, explains and will drive Jonathan's love of David and his betrayal of his father. (It will also, as we will see, cause Jonathan to parallel his father at the end as both die tragically in battle.) As I discussed earlier, God's rejection of Saul leads to Saul's betrayal of Jonathan with a vow that endangers him. Considering his father's action, Jonathan has good reason to fear and distrust Saul, and therefore to retaliate in kind. Who better to help with this retaliation than his kindred spirit—or, to use modern lingo, his possible twin flame, David?

The timeline of David and Jonathan's relationship shows that Saul's curse and betrayal is the central motivating factor that drives Jonathan and David together as loving allies and friends. As I discussed earlier, God's rejection of Saul in 1 Samuel 13 is followed by accounts of Jonathan's victories that suggest that the crown prince is likely Saul's replacement (1 Sam. 14:1–23). Immediately after this, Saul makes a vow, which disqualifies Jonathan (1 Sam. 14:24–45). This is succeeded by a second story of Saul's rejection (1 Sam. 15) where Samuel foretells that Saul's kingship will indeed end and that God will replace Saul with a *re'a*, which can be translated as "friend," "neighbor," or even, at times, tellingly, "paramour" (Song 5:16; Jer. 3:1, 20; Hos. 3:1). It is immediately after this second rejection that we meet David, a character whom everybody, including Jonathan and Saul, is said to *love*.[27] This introduction reveals that David is indeed the *re'a* who will replace Saul and that therefore Saul's curse has successfully disqualified Jonathan as Saul's possible

---

27. David is confirmed as this "friend" by Samuel after his death at 1 Sam. 28:17.

replacement. Moreover, the sequence of stories, whereby the vow is book-ended by the two stories of Saul's rejection, indicates that the vow and curse play a central role in the relationship between Jonathan and David, the two possible candidates to take over for Saul.

The background sets the scene for Jonathan's first meeting with David, which signals the beginning of their intense relationship: ". . . the soul [*nephesh*] of Jonathan was bound [*niqsherah*] to the soul [*nephesh*] of David, and Jonathan loved [*ahav*] him as his own soul [*nephesh*]. . . . Then Jonathan made a covenant with David because he loved [*ahav*] him as his own soul [*nephesh*]" (1 Sam. 18:1–3). These sentences are repeated later when David, now fleeing from Saul, meets with Jonathan, who warns David about Saul and makes another covenant with him: "Jonathan made David swear again by his love [*ahav*] for him; for he loved him as he loved [*ahav*] his own life [*nephesh*]" (1 Sam. 20:17).

This description as well as the sequence of events point to the unstated feelings and motivations that undergird the events. Wounded by his unloving father, who has been shown to be willing, perhaps even eager, to sacrifice him to stay in power, Jonathan desperately needs someone on his side, someone he can trust who can help him repay the machinations of his increasingly desperate father. He finds just such a friend in David, with whom he has much in common. Like Jonathan, David exhibits piety, is politically adept, and is capable on the battlefield. Jonathan no doubt likely feels a sense of kinship with David, especially as both he and David are justifiably wary of and will be victims of Saul's dangerous attempts to hold onto power (1 Sam. 19).

The repeated use of *nephesh*—a word that is usually translated as soul but can also mean mind, appetite, will, or life, as I explained earlier—lends further insight into the reasons behind the bond of these two characters. The statements that Jonathan's *nephesh* was bound to (*qashar*) David's *nephesh* (1 Sam. 18:1) or that Jonathan loved David as his own *nephesh* (1 Sam. 18:3; 20:17) equates and connects Jonathan's *nephesh* to that of David. Considering that David and Jonathan are depicted as having much the same regal attributes, it seems likely that these parallels have something to do with their similar or connected or bonded (*qashar*) *nephesh*-es.

The verb used to describe the connected relationship of the *nephesh*-es at 1 Samuel 18:1—*niqsharah* from the root *qashar*, usually translated as "bound"—speaks to the particular action that they will pursue together. Aside from "to bind," *qashar* can also mean "to conspire" or "to form a rebellion." That is, the term *qashar* can be a political term suggestive of rebellions or conspiracies against ruling monarchs (1 Sam. 22:8, 13; 1 Kgs. 15:27; 16:9, 16, 20; 2 Kgs. 9:14; 10:9; 12:20; 14:19; 15:10, 15, 25, 30; 21:23, 24). We see this at 1 Samuel 22:8 when Saul accuses his fellow Benjaminites of conspiring (*qashar*) against him by not informing him of the covenant between Jonathan and

David. Moreover, in 1 Samuel 22:13, Saul also accuses the priests at Nob, especially the head priest, Ahimelech—likely another relative of Saul's, as his name means "my brother is king"—for conspiring (*qashar*) against him and siding with David.

Considering the emphasis on *ahav* as well as the repeated use of *nephesh*, the political undertones of *qashar*, and the mention of two covenants between David and Jonathan, we can conclude that their love relationship centered on their conspiracy against Saul. In sum, Jonathan discovers that Saul is willing to kill him in order to stay in power by way of his father's vow and curse. Well aware of his father's faltering abilities and his rejection by God, and noticing his own popularity and potential, Jonathan decides not to play along. Fearful and vengeful, Jonathan encounters David, a man whose *nephesh*—which I take to mean his mind, ambition, and talent—matches his own. David also is a man on the make and therefore is the perfect ally with whom Jonathan can move against Saul. As a result, they decide to work together (*qasher*) to overthrow Saul, ratifying their agreement with a covenant—an item that, as we saw in the first chapter, is inextricably linked to love (*ahav*).

The first covenant is made right after they are introduced (1 Sam. 18:3), though what it entails is left unstated in the text. However, judging by the use of *nephesh*—here, shared political ambition and desires—I take it that the first covenant likely entails a mutually beneficial agreement concerning joint seditious activities. After David flees from Saul, Jonathan and David covertly meet and agree to a second covenant.[28] This second agreement clearly indicates that the two will work together to bring down Saul. By this point, it seems that Saul has uncovered some of their treasonous activities, which explains why David has been forced to go into hiding. In this second agreement, Jonathan promises to warn David if Saul tries to harm him (20:13), while David promises to treat Jonathan and his family kindly; that is, show them "the faithful love [*hesed*] of the LORD" (1 Sam. 20:14–15). All of this strongly suggests that Jonathan and David's agreement—and the love (*ahav*) between them—still centers on regime change, something which would endanger the royal family, including Jonathan.[29] As such, the love relationship between Jonathan and David stems from familial betrayal and lack of love: first Saul betrays Jonathan

28. The mention of the two "cutting a covenant," the doing of *hesed* or covenant loyalty (1 Sam. 20:14–15) as well as the use of the "language of a subordinate treaty partner," as David refers to himself as Jonathan's servant (*eved*) "suggests clearly that the love that accompanies these actions, and even prompts them, is covenant love" (Olyan, "'Surpassing the Love of Women,'" 8).

29. Jonathan seems to have put himself into quite a pickle. If Saul remains on the throne, and Jonathan's treasonous activities are discovered, he and his family would be endangered. If Saul, however, is deposed, Jonathan, as part of the royal family, would still be endangered. (Hence, the covenant with David.) The only way out for Jonathan was to become king himself,

and fails to love him, and Jonathan, in turn, betrays Saul and also fails to love him. Betrayals, however, are dicey and unstable, with a tendency to spur other acts of treachery, especially for those who love (*ahav*). Hence, the series of betrayals signals that more betrayals are to come.

DAVID'S BETRAYALS OF SAUL AND JONATHAN

Tellingly, it is not Jonathan but another character who will gain the most from Saul's downfall and the ensuing fragmentation of the royal family: David, who despite not being the royal heir, a blood relation of Saul's, or even a member of the same tribe, ends up king. That David, the character who is always the recipient but never the giver of love, would therefore emerge holding the prize is unsurprising. The love that David receives from everyone, as I argued above, in being connected to divine favoritism and power signals his fated rise.

Moreover, just as the lack of the mention of Saul's love for Jonathan signaled his forthcoming betrayal of his son, so also the lack of mention of love by David for either Saul or Jonathan—or anyone really—signals his likely betrayal of both figures. Indeed, considering the outcome, and considering the series of betrayals, it is unlikely that David remains innocent of treachery. If Jonathan can be charged with backstabbing his father, so we must also charge David, his partner, his "lover" or ally, with the same. We might even presume that because Saul is said to love David, but never said to love Jonathan, it is David's betrayal that is the more hurtful and meaningful of the two. David, after all, is taken into Saul's family, and the sick king comes to love and depend on him, especially as a source of relief from a divinely induced affliction (1 Sam. 16:21–23).

Even more egregious than David's backstabbing of Saul is his betrayal of Jonathan. Hinting of duplicity, David is oddly indisposed and unavailable during the battle in which Jonathan, David's "lover," is killed alongside his father and brothers. Though he does not have time to assist Jonathan on the battlefield, David does, however, find time to get wind of their demise from a messenger. Not only does this messenger just happen to know to go to David with this news, but he also does so bearing Saul's crown and armlet.[30] David's

---

an outcome that he seems to have realized was unlikely, considering his second covenant with David.

30. The events surrounding the death of Jonathan and his family are highly suspicious. During the battle in which Jonathan, David's "lover," is killed alongside his father and brothers, David just happens to be unavailable and dealing with a family crisis elsewhere: chasing after the Amalekites who have kidnapped his family (1 Sam. 30). The Amalekites seem to have

suspicious and treacherous behavior does not stop there. After Jonathan's death, despite David's promises in the second covenant that he will ensure the protection of Jonathan's family (1 Sam. 20:12–17), almost all the male heirs of Saul, likely including unnamed sons of Jonathan, eventually end up dead (2 Sam. 21). The only survivor is Jonathan's son, Mephibosheth, who likely survives because he is lame (2 Sam. 4:4) and therefore poses little threat to David (2 Sam. 9). As such, David appears to have so radically reinterpreted his covenant with Jonathan so as to render it meaningless.[31]

In hindsight, from the very beginning of Jonathan and David's relationship, there were hints that things would end badly. Immediately after they meet, 1 Samuel 18:3–4 states, "Then Jonathan made a covenant with David, because he loved him as his own soul. Jonathan stripped[32] himself of the robe that he was wearing, and gave it to David, and his armor, and even his sword and his bow and his belt." According to this passage, love drives Jonathan to give to David, someone whom he has just met, items that symbolize Jonathan's military and political power and status—his robe, armor, sword, bow, and belt. As if sensing the incomprehensibility of this action, especially by the usually astute and clever crown prince, the narrative deflects by using wordplay to bring out the theological significance of this transfer.[33] Befitting

---

been very busy during that time. Immediately after the battle concludes, another Amalekite runs to David to tell him of Saul's demise and to bring him Saul's crown and armlet. David rewards the poor messenger by killing him, using the Amalekite's assistance in Saul's death as a pretense (2 Sam. 1:1–16). Considering this strange and somewhat illogical sequence of events, it is hard not to conclude that the Amalekites are the fall guys for some unexplained act of treachery and murder on the part of David. They are the supposed reason why David could not participate in Israel's battle against its enemy and why he therefore could not come to the aid of his friend, Jonathan. An Amalekite is also, however, the means through which David gets news of Saul and Jonathan's deaths and takes control of the kingship. How and why an Amalekite—part of the group that kidnapped David's family—knows to go to David to report these deaths is not clear.

31. David remains true to his agreement with Jonathan to "never cut off your faithful love [*hesed*] from my house" (i.e., family) (1 Sam. 20:15), but only if by "house" or "family," and by "*hesed*," faithful love, what is meant is keeping just one son—the least dangerous and most vulnerable—of Jonathan's alive and under close watch while murdering the rest.

32. Yaron Peleg argues that the word here (root *pashat*) also implies the sexual subjugation of Jonathan as he is depicted as taking off "the signs of his authority and manhood" in a submissive manner (Yaron Peleg, "Love at First Sight? David, Jonathan, and the Biblical Politics of Gender," *Journal for the Study of the Old Testament* 30, no. 2 [2005]: 171–89, [181]).

33. That Jonathan would hand over to someone he has just met the keys to the kingdom, no matter how intense the love, makes little sense considering the portrayal of this character thus far in the narrative. As I discussed, Jonathan is depicted as soldierly, circumspect, and ambitious. He knows, as the crown prince, that he is the rightful heir to Saul's throne, and indeed, the tension with his father seems to center on his desire to ascend the throne more quickly, not to hand it over to someone else. Even if we assume that Jonathan has accepted his disqualification due to his contravention of his father's vow, why would Jonathan hand over to David—whom he has just met—the kingship ahead of time, before really seeing where the

his name, Jonathan, whose name means "gift of YHWH" or "YHWH gives," hands over to David the very symbols of his royal authority. Jonathan, the "gift of YHWH" or "YHWH gives," therefore, serves as YHWH's proxy to give to YHWH's favored David the throne that was originally meant for Jonathan. That Jonathan, after removing and giving to David all his accoutrement, resembles a prisoner or captive hints of his victimhood, both in the unfolding tragedy fated for him and his family, and also of love, which has ominous connections.

As such, it is hard to deny that the portrayal of David and Jonathan's relationship, especially the repeated mention of Jonathan's love of David, has propagandistic purposes: to explain why David ascended the throne instead of David's "lover" Jonathan. Even the portrayal of the two characters as doubles serves to justify David's double-dealing: as doubles and as Jonathan's beloved, the implication is that Jonathan and David are so similar that the two should really be viewed as essentially equivalent—nearly interchangeable. Technically Jonathan never gets to rule; yet he comes close through the reign of his twin, David. Instead of the reign of the talented Jonathan, the crown prince, the legitimate heir to the Saulide throne, Israel instead gets the next best thing—something like the reign of Jonathan only enacted through the body of Jonathan's beloved, David.

Once our eyes are open to David's treacherous nature, even David's lament after he learns of the deaths of Saul and Jonathan in 2 Samuel 1 appears shady and encoded in doublespeak. Initially, this lament seems to be a beautiful cri de coeur by a bereaved friend or even, as some argue, a bereaved lover. Indeed, so persuasive is David's lament that interpreters wonder whether the mention of Jonathan's love as "wonderful, passing the love of women" (2 Sam. 1:26) hints of a homoerotic or romantic relationship between the two.[34]

Yet a closer look at this lament, especially the nuances of the terms and the wordplay, brings out the darker insinuations of the poem. Take, for example, 2 Samuel 1:23 where David states, "Saul and Jonathan, beloved [*han-ne'ehavim*, from *ahav*] and lovely! In life and in death they were not divided; they were swifter [*qalal*] than eagles, they were stronger [*gavar*] than lions." Initially, these lines sound like your typical exaggerated praise for the deceased. However, the extent of the exaggeration and falsehood is notable and, therefore,

---

chips fall? No matter how impressive or taken Jonathan is with David, who is portrayed as very similar to him, handing over the symbols of his royal status so quickly would be unwise considering that a usurper (which is what David is) would endanger the well-being of the entire royal family, including Jonathan's own siblings and children.

34. Olyan, "'Surpassing the Love of Women,'" 7–16. Contra Diana Vikander ("The Authenticity of 2 Samuel 1.26 in the Lament over Saul and Jonathan," *Scandinavian Journal of the Old Testament* 2, no. 1 [1988]: 66–75), who argues that the love here speaks of political alliance.

fishy. The statement that Saul and Jonathan were beloved seems to go against the preceding narrative where Saul and Jonathan are never said to be loved by anyone, not even by each other and certainly not by David. Though the absence of love for Saul and Jonathan does not necessarily mean David's statement is false, the mention of love by David is suspicious, especially when we consider that the only person who is loved, repeatedly and empathetically, in the text is David.

Equally ludicrous is David's statement that father and son were not divided in life or in death (2 Sam. 1:23). While it is true that they are united in death in so far as they both die during the same battle, surely the same cannot be said about father and son "in life" considering that most of 1 Samuel centers on their disagreements, betrayals, and eventual disunity. Rather, the only thing that seems to have united Jonathan and Saul, at least briefly, is their conjoined love of David—a mutual love that later served as the source of further fragmentation of father and son (1 Sam. 20).

The falsehoods indicate that something is off about David's lament. If we interpret this lament more suspiciously, the tone of it does not necessarily seem altogether sorrowful. Rather, David seems to be boasting, almost taunting the just-fallen pair by slyly hinting of the betrayals between father and son— betrayals that David fomented and took advantage of during his rise to the top. For example, David declares in 2 Samuel 1:23 that Jonathan and Saul were "swifter [qalal] than eagles" and "stronger [gavar] than lions." Not only is this statement untrue considering that Saul and Jonathan are now both dead, and so apparently not as quick or strong as they needed to be, but it also subtly alludes to events that led to their fallen state. The Hebrew term for "swift" or "quick"—qal from the root qalal—can also mean "to diminish, dishonor, despise" (Gen. 16:4, 5; 2 Sam. 6:22; 19:43; Isa. 23:9; Nah. 1:14) or "curse" (Job 24:18; Ps. 37:22; Isa. 65:20). Hence, by saying qalal, David seems to be subtly referring not to their quickness but to God's rejection and betrayal of Saul, which led to his diminishment, dishonor, and likely demise. Additionally, again through the use of qalal, David subtly alludes to Saul's betrayal of Jonathan: that is, Saul's vow and curse of Jonathan, a factor that likely led to Jonathan's own death as well as his love of David and his betrayal of his father.

Similarly, gavar, which is translated as "stronger," can also mean "to prevail." Given that Saul and Jonathan have just been killed in battle, that is, have just failed to prevail against their enemies, it makes little sense to laud them as being "stronger than lions." Rather, by stating something untrue, David, through the lament, draws attention to the person who has been shown to be the truly quick, the truly strong, the truly beloved—the one who has truly prevailed—that is, David. It is David, the lament declares (and celebrates), not Jonathan and Saul, who is loved (ahav), who is quick, and who is strong—and therefore who has prevailed (gavar) against the diminished, despised, dishonored, divided, and cursed, that is *qalal*, Saul and Jonathan. David does not lament the death of Saul and Jonathan so much as gloat over his triumph over his hoodwinked "lovers."[35]

THE PAIN AND MYSTERY OF LOVE

The stories we examined in this chapter show that love is a source of great pain and suffering, especially, though not exclusively, for the unloved. As we saw with Esau and Saul, a lack of love can cause emotional devastation. Jonathan is no different. The lack of love from his father drives Jonathan to betray Saul by aligning himself with David. The lack of love also opens up Jonathan to love David. Hence, love, or the lack of love, in the cases of Jonathan and Saul, make them vulnerable to a manipulator who has little qualms over taking advantage of their heartache.

Considering the pain that follows from the absence of love, which in turn stems from God's preferences, every story that we have explored thus far raises the same challenging question: Why does God allow the beloved character he prefers to take such egregious advantage of the unloved characters? In the case of Esau and Saul, the previous chapters offered some plausible explanations. Jonathan's case, however, is by far more distressing. Unlike Saul, Jonathan commits no wrongdoing, is faithful and capable, and appears popular with everyone except his father. Jonathan, as I argued, might even have been initially selected by God to be Saul's replacement. Why then does Jonathan, who is portrayed as better than his father, succumb to the same tragic fate? Even if we can explain Jonathan's death and failure as due to Saul's foolish vow, the theological difficulties remain as this explanation fails to address why God allows David to take advantage of Jonathan: Why does God remain silent while Jonathan, who loves and trusts David, is exploited and manipulated by him?

Though the text never directly answers these questions, we can infer something approaching an explanation by looking more closely at those whom God does favor: Jacob and David. Tellingly, these two characters share similarities that shed light on God's mysterious preferences. Like Jacob, who is the eponymous ancestor of Israel, so David can also be said to represent and symbolize the nation-state, especially the southern kingdom of Judah. David, after all, is not just Israel's best-known and most successful king, but he establishes

---

35. David G. Firth implies this when he argues that 1 Sam. 27–2 Sam. 1 should be considered the accession narrative of David (David G. Firth, "The Accession Narrative (1 Samuel 27–2 Samuel 1)," *Tyndale Bulletin* 58, no. 1 [2007]: 61–81).

Jerusalem/Zion as the nation's capital and founds the country's only royal dynasty.[36]

Additionally, just as Jacob might have been unusually close to God, David too might be envisioned as a particular favorite. It is telling that when God makes a covenant with David in 2 Samuel 7, God tells David, using the adoption formula, that "I will be a father to him [David's descendant], and he shall be a son to me" (2 Sam. 7:14). Though this language of adoption is used in particular types of ancient Near Eastern covenants called covenants of grant,[37] this type of promise undoubtedly speaks to a special closeness, even approaching a kind of kinship between God and David (and his descendants).

Considering that both Jacob and David make special covenants with God and are even intimated as part of God's family, it might be that God particularly favors them because they represent Israel. God's love of Israel, which is repeatedly stated in the Hebrew text (Deut. 10:15; Ps. 130:7; Hos. 11:1; Jer. 31:3; Isa. 43:1, 4; 54:10), is therefore mirrored in God's love of Jacob/Israel and David—two characters who act as stand-ins for the nation. As we have said before, so again the meaning of David's name—"beloved"—is shown to be both fitting and prescient. Hence, God allows David's ruthless, treacherous, and likely bloody actions, even against the innocent Jonathan, because God loves David and prefers him. And God does so because God mysteriously loves and prefers Israel, which David comes to represent.

An example later in the text reveals the extent of God's love. When David is king, he infamously impregnates a married woman named Bathsheba and then murders her husband (2 Sam. 11)—a wrongdoing far more egregious than any committed by Saul. So strong is God's love of Israel/David and so enamored is he of David that even after this brutal act, God still refrains from removing the crown or dynasty from David. Indeed, David is not even really punished, at least not directly. Rather, the brunt of the punishment is borne by David's children (2 Sam. 12:13–19).

This is, to be sure, hardly David's only transgression. Considering that David is only ever punished lightly, if at all, for his many wrongdoings, God's love of David, as shown in his willingness to forgive and indulge David, is depicted as illogical and mysterious. It is also seemingly limitless. So powerful a force is love that it is able to sway God—to cause God to turn a blind eye to the egregious offenses of his beloved. Moreover, that there is no explanation for the reason behind God's love of these troublesome figures suggests that God, himself, does not fully understand why he loves who he does and

36. Bespeaking David's national importance, it is the star of David or the shield of David (*magen David*) that serves as the emblem on the flag of the modern state of Israel.

37. Moshe Weinfeld, "The Covenant of Grant in the Old Testament and in the Ancient Near East," *Journal of the American Oriental Society* 90, no. 2 (1970): 184–203.

why he continues to love them despite their distressing actions. Considering love's hold over God, this powerful force seems to vie with God himself for supremacy. This problematic idea—that love might be something equal to or perhaps even more powerful than God—as we will see in the next chapter, deepens the question of what, or who, love is.

CONCLUSION

As we saw in the previous chapter, God's anguish at being rejected by Israel led to his actions against Saul, whom he quickly selects, rejects, and then secretly replaces as king. Saul, the victim of love, in turn, continues the cycle of abuse by lashing out against Jonathan, his firstborn son. Jonathan, like his father before him, finds solace in David, whom he is said to love and with whom he makes two covenants, likely concerning the overthrow of Saul. Perhaps these agreements entailed David becoming second in command once Jonathan, the crown prince, ascended the throne. Jonathan, however, appears to have miscalculated and misjudged the ambitious ruthlessness of his supposed ally. Whatever the agreements between David and Jonathan might have been, at the end, Saul and all of his sons, including Jonathan, end up dead.

Love is key to this tragedy. Though Jonathan and David initially appear similar, as shown by their varying fates, they could hardly be more different. Rather one key thing sets them apart: the love of Saul and, by extension, the love of God. This love not only separates Jonathan and David, but it reveals the parallels between Saul and Jonathan. Despite their initial contrasts, both father and son end up dead on the same battlefield at the same time—deserted and betrayed by their beloved, David. Considering David's lament, which seems heavily laden with hidden meaning, it seems likely that David, however he might have felt about Saul and Jonathan, was ultimately comfortable with using their love against them. When given a chance to stab Jonathan and Saul in the back, David appears to have had no qualms about doing so.

In its ability and potential to cause suffering, love is depicted as a source of incredible power. This power, as shown by David, can be manipulated, however. Love can be used as a tool by the ruthless and power-hungry to sow discord, to foment division, and to obtain power by betraying others. As such, the issues we have explored in the previous two chapters—the divinity of love and the power of love—intersect with the topic of this chapter: the pain and mystery of love. This, in turn, leads to other questions, which we will explore in the final chapter: If love is divine and powerful, so much so that it can move God, who or what is in control of this power? What divine force is so powerful that it is capable of affecting God? God's unstated but obvious love of David, and David's ability to manipulate those who love him, begin to suggest that love is its own entity, a power separate from God that seems to hold sway over him. If so, what—or who—is love?

5

The Gender of Love

Women and Love

INTRODUCTION

The stories we have explored depict love as a divine phenomenon of great potency, capable of causing tremendous suffering and pain. So great is power of love that even God seems to be carried along by its strange logic. In this final chapter, we attempt to come to a better understanding of this divine, powerful, mysterious, and sometimes painful thing called love by exploring the gender implications of love. We do so by examining stories from the Hebrew text that mention love in connection with women. We turn first to the unfortunate tales of Michal, Rebekah, and Ruth, who, outside the Song of Songs, are the three other female characters in the Hebrew Bible who are said to love someone. Not coincidentally, they all have unlucky outcomes as a result of their love. Next, we examine the horrific stories of the rapes of Dinah and of Tamar, both of whom are disturbingly said to have been loved by their rapists and whose fates are left unfinished and unwritten in the text. Lastly, we conclude with a discussion on how these lethal visions of love find their apotheosis in the Song of Songs, a unique book in the Hebrew Bible in that it explores and indeed celebrates erotic and sexual love.

Through this exploration of these tragic and painful stories about women and love, we discover that love itself might be imagined as a woman. Yet because of love's great power and potential for chaos, great enough even to affect and influence God, the Hebrew text suppresses the gender of love. This suppression, furthermore, takes several overlapping forms: First, and most generally, by depicting love in connection with women as negative; second, by undermining and suppressing women's ability to love; and third, through the enactment of violence and abuse on women who love and are loved. Despite this attempt to silence, suppress, and erase, the text inadvertently, however, cannot help but disclose and acknowledge love's deep connection to women and, in so doing, appears to suggest that love itself should be imagined as female.

WOMEN AS ACTIVE SUBJECTS OF LOVE

Aside from the Song of Songs, which, as I explain later is a unique book, the Hebrew text mentions only three other women characters who actively love someone: Rebekah loves Jacob (Gen. 25:28); Michal loves David (1 Sam. 18:20); and Ruth loves Naomi (Ruth 4:15). This paucity of female characters who are said to love cannot be because women are incapable of love or tend to love less frequently or passionately.[1] So why does the Hebrew Bible want to deny this basic human impulse? That is, why are women, when it comes to love, so infrequently the active "lover"? Were men thought more capable of love in some way in the ancient Near East and, therefore, does the Hebrew Bible reflect this context? The answer to this last question might be a qualified yes. That is, male characters are perhaps envisioned as more able to love—to be the lover, as it were—in the Hebrew text. Some of this has to do with the particular history and focus of this text. Written and edited by male scribes, the Hebrew Bible is a product of, by, and for men. Therefore, women and children and other groups that do not fit into this narrowly defined category inevitably find less representation and consideration.

However, this cannot be the only reason why women are so infrequently portrayed as the active lovers in the text. As is evident from the few examples of the female characters who do love, this idea is possible, just rare. Indeed, not only does the rarity of females who love hint that there might be something peculiar and special about these particular figures, but it also undoubtedly suggests (again) that love is understood differently in the ancient text.

Biblical scholar Susan Ackerman addresses this very issue by turning to William Moran's idea that *ahav*, because of its use in covenants or ancient treaties,

---

1. In fact, I would venture that right now, at least in the United States, the opposite stereotype pertains. That is, women, more than men, are associated with love, especially romantic love. Indeed, Francesca M. Cancian describes the economic processes behind the feminization of love in the United States. Connected to emotions and powerlessness, love became increasingly associated with women, while in contrast men were associated with love's opposites: work and skill. See Francesca M. Cancian, "The Feminization of Love," *Signs: Journal of Women in Culture and Society* 11, no. 4 (1986): 692–709.

was centrally a political term.[2] Ackerman argues that because of this close connection between love and covenants, specifically covenants made between a lesser and greater entity (i.e., suzerain-vassal treaties), *ahav* has connotations of power.[3] Hence, who gets to be the subject of *ahav* and who gets to be the object of it depends on where each are positioned in the social hierarchy: How much power an individual has relative to the other person determines whether they are the subject or object of love. Thus, the reason why only Rebekah, Michal, and Ruth are the subjects and not objects of love is because these women, despite their gender, are hierarchically higher in some way and in a greater position of power over the characters whom they are said to love.[4]

REBEKAH LOVES JACOB

Ackerman gives us a good starting point to examine these female characters and their love in more detail. We begin with Rebekah, a character with whom we have spent some time in chapter 2. Rebekah is said to love only one of her twins, Jacob, while her husband, Isaac, in contrast, is said to love only the other twin, Esau (Gen. 25:28). While the statement that Isaac loves his son is unsurprising considering that he as a patriarch would sit at the top of the social hierarchy, the statement that Rebekah, Isaac's wife, loves Jacob is unusual considering her gender (Gen. 25:28). Ackerman explains that Rebekah is portrayed as the subject because, though she is a woman, she is also Jacob's mother. And as a parent, Rebekah is hierarchically higher than Jacob, the object of love. Children, Ackerman notes, are never said to love anyone in the Hebrew text, including their parents, not because they are incapable of love, but because children did not have enough power and therefore social standing to be considered as the subject of love.

Though Ackerman's conclusions are convincing, there might be another reason, related to gender, that makes Rebekah's love of Jacob unique. Yes, Rebekah's love of one of her twin sons is odd in that she is a female character. But her love is also doubly strange because her love of Jacob is in diametric opposition to Isaac's love of Esau. Considering that Isaac is a patriarch of Israel—indeed, the near sacrificed, elect son of Abraham (Gen. 22)—the expectation would be that Isaac's love of Esau would override or cancel Rebekah's love of Jacob. After all, despite Rebekah's travails of pregnancy,

2. William Moran, "The Ancient Near Eastern Background of the Love of God in Deuteronomy," *Catholic Biblical Quarterly* 25, no. 1 (1963): 77–87.

3. Susan Ackerman, "The Personal Is Political: Covenantal and Affectionate Love (*'aheb, 'ahaba*) in the Hebrew Bible," *Vetus Testamentum* 52, fasc. 4 (2002): 437–58.

4. Ackerman, "Personal Is Political," 437–58.

patriarch still trumps matriarch in the Hebrew text. Yet strangely this is not what happens. Rather, it is peculiar that God seems to agree, at least passively, with Rebekah's preference for her younger twin, standing by while she and Jacob take advantage of both Isaac and Esau (Gen. 27). Bespeaking further support, God in a later theophany even appears to Jacob to affirm that he is indeed the inheritor of God's promises to Abraham (Gen. 28:10–22). Thus, by all appearances, God seems to side with Rebekah and her choice over against that of Isaac, the patriarch.

God's concurrence with Rebekah explains why her love prevails over that of Isaac. Despite Isaac being a patriarch and therefore higher than Rebekah on the social ladder, he is lower hierarchically than the ultimate patriarch, God. And God, for reasons I discussed in chapter 2, sides with Rebekah. Hence, while Rebekah is depicted as one of the rare female characters to actively love, in part because of her position as a parent, her love is depicted as overriding the contrasting love of Isaac because it is affirmed by the male deity YHWH, who has final say.

Initially, God's agreement with Rebekah's love of Jacob seems positive in the narrative. It appears that there is divine and therefore textual affirmation of the love choices and preferences of female characters. However, the depiction of God's affirmation of Rebekah's love of Jacob can be read as conveying quite the opposite meaning: as reflective of a discomfort with female characters being the subjects and not the objects of love. The affirmation of God, a male character, of the love of Rebekah, a female character, undercuts and undermines her power and authority as the active subject of love as her preferences and love are deemed valid mainly because an important male character, God, agrees with her. The idea that the power of *ahav* is the prerogative of males and that it is males, not females, who ought to be the real subject of *ahav* is reconfirmed.

This discomfort with a female character as the subject of love might also explain the tragic conclusion that results from Rebekah's love of Jacob. As I mentioned in chapter 2, Rebekah's love for Jacob, which leads her to help him steal the blessing meant for Esau, results in Jacob's flight from Canaan (Gen. 27:41–45). As a result, Rebekah never sees her favorite son again. Because of her love, Rebekah suffers and tragically loses her beloved child forever. While Rebekah certainly is not the only character to suffer because of her love in the Hebrew text—her son Jacob will tragically lose the wife he loves, Rachel, prematurely as well (Gen. 35:16–20)—it is difficult to shake the feeling that the tragic consequences of Rebekah's love entail a deliberate act of narrative retribution. For daring to love and for daring to act on her love, Rebekah is punished with the eternal separation and loss of the object of her love.

MICHAL LOVES DAVID

The tragic story about Michal, the daughter of Saul and sister of Jonathan—another rare female character who is made the subject of love (1 Sam. 18:20)—reflects similar unease and ambivalence. Considering that Michal's introduction (1 Sam. 14:49) follows fast upon the heels of her father's curse of Jonathan for a broken vow—a brother who is figured almost as Michal's twin—the narrative foreshadows a disastrous future for the princess.

Love again is presented as a marker of and connected to her looming tragedy. Like her ill-fated brother, Michal too is said to love David (1 Sam. 18:20), and as a result of her love, is given by Saul to David as his wife (1 Sam. 18:27). Thinking again of love as part and parcel of status, Jonathan's love of David makes perfect sense: Jonathan is the crown prince and therefore of higher social standing than David. Ackerman explains Michal's love of David similarly: Though Michal is female, she is permitted to be the subject of love as she is a princess, and therefore of a higher rank than David who, at this point in the narrative, is just an army commander (and maybe Saul's personal music therapist).[5]

However, as with Rebekah, the portrayal of Michal, particularly in her depiction as a female double of her brother, Jonathan, reflects ambivalent understandings of love and gender. The similarities between Michal and Jonathan are worth nothing. Emphasizing doubles, Michal is also said to love David like Jonathan (1 Sam. 18:20). Moreover, both Michal and Jonathan are associated with the defeat of the Philistines. Jonathan goes on a successful solo mission against the Philistines in 1 Samuel 14 while David's bride-price for Michal as determined by Saul is, gruesomely, one hundred foreskins of the Philistines. (David, ever the overachiever, delivers *double* that number to Saul [1 Sam. 18:25–27].) Both siblings also make covenants with David. Indeed, Jonathan makes *two* covenants with David (1 Sam. 18:3; 20:18), while Michal, in that she marries David, is part of a marriage contract or covenant (1 Sam. 18:27). Both of Saul's children side with their beloved David over against their father, going so far as to help David escape his clutches.[6] The Hebrew text parallels Jonathan and Michal's actions in helping David escape by using the same three verbs—"slipped, fled, and escaped" (19:10 and 19:12).[7]

5. Ackerman, "Personal Is Political," 452–53.
6. In 2 Samuel 19:1–10, Jonathan warns David that Saul is trying to kill him. And when Saul, filled with the evil spirit of YHWH, later throws a spear at David, Michal helps David escape the palace by dressing up and placing in bed a humanoid household figurine called a teraphim to mimic David's presence (2 Sam. 19:11–17).
7. Yaron Peleg, "Love at First Sight? David, Jonathan, and the Biblical Politics of Gender," *Journal for the Study of the Old Testament* 30, no. 2 (2005): 171–89 (187).

Both children of Saul also share similarities with their ancestress, Rachel, including a lethal family curse.[8] Rachel struggles to have children and dies while giving birth to her second son, Benjamin (Gen. 35:18). Her eldest son, Joseph, moreover, is sold by his brothers and exiled to Egypt for most of his life (Gen. 37, 39–50), exile being a well-known metaphor for death in the Hebrew text.[9] As I discussed, Jonathan, a descendant of Rachel, ends up prematurely dying alongside Saul and his other brothers during a battle with the Philistines (1 Sam. 31), and all of Jonathan's sons, except one, Mephibosheth, are eventually killed (2 Sam. 4:4; 9; 21), probably at the unstated behest of David.

Michal suffers a similar fate, albeit metaphoric. When David consolidates his rule, he forces Michal to be returned to him as his wife, likely to legitimize his kingship by claiming kinship to the preceding king, Saul (1 Sam. 3:13–16). Michal understandably is not thrilled to be forcibly returned to the man who is responsible for the demise of her family and their fall from power. And when she sees David dancing at a celebration of the entrance of the ark into the new capital, Jerusalem, an event that also marks the consolidation of David's rule, she criticizes him for his shameless dancing (2 Sam. 6:20–23). For this criticism, David cuttingly tells her that he is dancing joyously for God, the deity who has chosen him to be king in the place of Michal's father. For daring to say something unkind to David, the text punishes Michal with something similar to death: "And Michal the daughter of Saul had no child to the day of her death" (2 Sam. 6:23).

Regardless of whether Michal's childlessness stems from her understandable disdain for David or from David's lack of a desire to help create a half-Saulide competitor to the throne, it is significant that Michal's fate metaphorically mirrors that of Jonathan. While Jonathan literally dies, so also Michal undergoes something akin to death in that she bears no children.[10] Hence both Michal and Jonathan suffer tragic, premature "deaths" and loss of descendants, likely because of their relationship to Saul, who also ends up dead. And

8. Like Jonathan, Michal too is likened to their ancestress Rachel. Not only is Michal, like Rachel, referred to as the "littler daughter," *qetannah* (1 Sam. 14:49; Gen. 29:16), but she, like Rachel, also uses a teraphim in an inappropriate manner. While Michal dresses up a teraphim to help David escape, Rachel steals and then sits on a teraphim, maybe while menstruating (Gen. 31:19, 35). As a result of her theft, Rachel is cursed by her husband Jacob and later dies as a result (Gen. 31:32; 35:16–18)—a tragedy that, as I briefly noted in a previous chapter, will be reenacted by her descendant, Jonathan, who is also cursed by a family member, his father, Saul (1 Sam. 14:24–46).

9. Jon D. Levenson, *Resurrection and the Restoration of Israel: The Ultimate Victory of the God of Life* (New Haven: Yale University Press, 2008).

10. In some translations and manuscripts of the Bible, Michal does have children (2 Sam. 21:8).

all three Saulides therefore mimic the fate of their ancestress Rachel and, in so doing, seem to be victims of the same unstated family curse.[11]

These similarities between Michal and her brother Jonathan again express unease about and subvert Michal's role and power as the subject of *ahav*. As scholars have noted, the parallels between Michal and Jonathan confuse the gender characterizations by feminizing Jonathan and masculinizing Michal.[12] Adele Berlin, for example, states that David relates to Michal, who is depicted as "aggressive and physical," as a man, and relates to Jonathan as a woman.[13] Tamara Eskenazi also notes that rabbis, noticing and stressing Michal's masculine depiction, mention her doing exclusively male activities, such as wearing phylacteries (*tephillin*) and studying the Torah.[14] Yaron Peleg also observes that "Jonathan is portrayed as passive and feminine and Michal is portrayed as aggressive and masculine."[15] He goes further and argues that these inverted gendered depictions are politically motivated: The reverse gendering of brother and sister delegitimates Jonathan as being too womanly to become king and, in contrast, legitimates David as a man who is manly enough to become the next monarch.[16]

Designating traits as more befitting of one gender or another is tricky business, of course, and the reader has to take care not to lapse into stereotypes. Hence, I remain unconvinced that Jonathan is portrayed as passive, and whether, even if he were, passivity should necessarily be envisioned as a *feminine* trait considering that several female characters in the Hebrew Bible are depicted as prodigiously active.[17] Moreover, as I noted in the previous chapter, Jonathan is depicted as a skilled fighter—a characteristic linked to masculinity in the ancient Near East—and is said to be generally quite active,

---

11. Indeed, the sounds of Michal's name hint of a curse. Her name is usually taken as a shortened form of *mi-ka-el*, that is, "Who is like El or God." However, *kal* is a homonym for another verb—*qalal*—which means "to make light or fun of," "to despise," "to show contempt," or, most importantly, "to curse." As such, Michal's name also sounds like: "Who or what curses" or "Who or what is cursed?"

12. Adele Berlin, "Characterization in Biblical Narrative: David's Wives," *Journal for the Study of the Old Testament* 23 (1982): 69–85; Peleg, "Love at First Sight?," 171–89.

13. Berlin, "Characterization," 71.

14. Tamara Eskenazi, "Michal in Hebrew Sources," in *Telling Queen Michal's Story: An Experiment in Comparative Interpretation*, ed. David J.A. Clines and Tamara C. Eskenazi (Sheffield: Sheffield Academic, 1991), 157–74 (158).

15. Peleg, "Love at First Sight?," 187

16. Peleg, "Love at First Sight?," 172.

17. Contra Peleg, many female characters in the Hebrew Bible, such as Sarah (Gen. 16, 21), Rebekah (Gen. 25:19–28, 27:1–46), Rachel (Gen. 30:1–24; 31:19), and Hannah (1 Sam. 1:1–2:10), are depicted as very active, perhaps too active, especially in contrast to their oddly passive male counterparts.

especially in his aid of David.[18] As the subject, not object, of love, Jonathan therefore is envisioned by the biblical authors as occupying the higher, more powerful—that is, masculine—position in the social hierarchy, something which would be expected of a male character, especially a royal one. Thus, I see little evidence of the feminization of Jonathan.

Michal, however, is a different, more complicated character. And discerning whether Michal abides by or deviates from expected gender expectations and characterizations is far trickier, particularly given that she is depicted as very similar to her brother Jonathan. Like Jonathan, Michal too is portrayed as an active ally and "lover" of David. Moreover, considering her similarities to her brother, her love of David must be motivated, at least partially, by her ambition.[19] Being a keen political strategist like her brother, Michal sides with her promising husband over against her declining father. Had Michal produced a son with David, the chances of their child becoming the future monarch of Israel were not insignificant, especially once the dust cleared from the battle between her husband and her father.

Considering these parallels between Jonathan and Michal, the question is whether activity, ambition, political astuteness, being in a position of power, and being the subject of love are envisioned as masculine traits in the Hebrew text. Unfortunately, the answer to this question likely is yes. Considering that male characters are usually the ones in positions of power and therefore usually depicted as upfront, direct engagers of political contests in the Hebrew text (though, as we see from Esther, female political engagement is not entirely lacking, just usually more hidden), it does seem that political power and activity are largely viewed as masculine attributes. Hence, though it is unlikely that Jonathan is feminized, it is likely that Michal's similarities with her brother depict her as acting more masculine.

Yet if Michal is indeed depicted as masculine, then the text ultimately undermines her exceptionalism and punishes her for being actively engaged in politics and love. As we have seen, her ability to love stems not solely from her royal status but also from her similarity to her brother Jonathan. That is, though she is a female character, she is "allowed" to be the subject of love because she, though a woman, parallels and acts like another man—Jonathan. Love—or at least, in terms of who has the power to give it or be the subject of

---

18. Cynthia R. Chapman, *The Gendered Language of Warfare in the Israelite-Assyrian Encounter,* Harvard Semitic Monographs 62 (Winona Lake: Eisenbrauns, 2004), esp. 20–59, 83. And not only is Jonathan the one who loves David—and not the reverse—but he also saves him from his father and makes two covenants with him.

19. Wilda Gafney writes, "Michal seems to be a fool for risking her privilege, status, and relationship with her father—if she ever had one—for a man who does not love, want, value, or miss her" (*Womanist Midrash: A Reintroduction to the Women of the Torah and the Throne* [Louisville: Westminster John Knox Press, 2017], 194).

it—again is shown to be largely the domain of men. This, we will note, closely aligns her with Rebekah, whose active love was permitted on the association with a male character, God.

This discomfort with female characters being the subjects of love also explains Michal's tragic fate as she, like Rebekah, will pay a price for her love. While Rebekah loses her beloved son, Michal suffers the near total loss of her family, many of whom die because of her husband and former object of her love, David. She will also suffer the loss of a family lineage as she is forcibly returned to David only to be caged and used as a political tool. Hence, like Rebekah, Michal pays for her love by losing the very thing she desires: political power for her and her descendants. The victim of David and the text, Michal, in the end, will be put in a position where she will never again be the subject of love.

RUTH LOVES NAOMI

We now turn to the most exceptional of exceptional cases: the one female character who is said to love another female character in the Hebrew Bible; that is, Ruth, who is indirectly said to love her mother-in-law, Naomi (Ruth 4:15). It is interesting that out of the three women who are said to love in the Hebrew Bible, Ruth has the most positive outcome. This might hint that the writers were slightly more comfortable with women loving other women, at least judging by the conclusion offered in this one exceptional case.

In four short chapters, the book of Ruth describes a Moabitess named Ruth who marries an Israelite man living in Moab who dies. Following shortly thereafter the deaths of the remaining men of this immigrant Israelite family, Ruth returns with her mother-in-law, Naomi, to Israel, Naomi's homeland. Impoverished, she resorts to gleaning until eventually, with the help of Naomi, she gets Boaz, a relative of her deceased husband, to perform Levirate marriage and become a kinsman redeemer. This institution, which is not fully understood, entails the brother of the deceased man to impregnate the widow and have a son in the name of the deceased. The story of Ruth is positively spun as a tale of rags-to-riches: Ruth and, by extension, Naomi, goes from being a poor, landless widow to a matriarch of a very important Israelite family.

The mention of love occurs in the aftermath of the story, right before the readers are told that the son born to Ruth will be the forefather of King David. Before we are told of the important destiny and patrilineal descent of this child, a group of women who act as the chorus throughout the book surround Naomi and give a blessing to her and her grandson, saying, "Blessed be the LORD, who has not left you this day without next-of-kin, and may his name be renowned in Israel! He shall be to you a restorer of life and a nourisher of your old age, for your daughter-in-law who *loves* you, who is more to you than seven sons, has borne him" (Ruth 4:14–16; emphasis added).

As with the two other cases, Susan Ackerman explains the statement about Ruth's love as indicative of her higher status.[20] As the mother of a son who will inherit land in Israel, Ruth is socially higher than Naomi, a poor, elderly widow. However, unique features of the Ruth story complicate Ackerman's conclusion. The main particularity is that this is the only time where both the subject and object of *ahav* are female, and as such, there is no other example with which to compare it. Any conclusion we draw about love, therefore, remains somewhat speculative. Adding to difficulties, Ruth, who is the rare female subject of love, is not stated to love Naomi directly. That is, the reader is never told directly by either the narrator or by Ruth of Ruth's motivations or whether she loves Naomi. Rather, the statement of her love is given by other women, Naomi's friends. It is they who declare how Ruth loves Naomi as she has provided her a grandson and, in doing so, is better than seven sons (Ruth 4:15).

This statement by the women reflects interesting conflicting feelings and messages. These women are celebrating the birth of an important male child, one who can continue the lineage and inherit, and therefore presumably provide for these impoverished women. Considering the emphasis on the maleness, the gender, of this child, it is ironic that the women claim that Ruth, a foreign, albeit loyal, daughter-in-law is better than any male heirs, indeed, seven such heirs (4:15). As Ruth and Naomi would not be in this fix had one of them just given birth to a single male child who lived, it is difficult to gauge the tone of this triumphant declaration. Clearly, the women are celebrating the survival of a woman—Naomi—and her family, one which miraculously comes about through the efforts of another woman, Ruth. Yet considering that all of it depends on the birth of a son, their message about the usefulness of Ruth is, interestingly, problematized. Ruth is important insofar as she gives birth to a male heir, one who, as the genealogical list that succeeds this celebration indicates, goes on to survive and produce more male descendants.

Related to this ambivalence, there is another strange aspect to the ending of Ruth. For all the celebratory declaration by these women of the value and love of Ruth for Naomi, Ruth herself disappears at the end of this tale. For some reason, it is not Ruth, but her mother-in-law, Naomi, who winds up being the main focus of the celebration at the end (Ruth 4:14–17).[21] Moreover, Naomi herself does not remain in the spotlight long as she too is sidelined, perhaps by a subsequent editor, by the addition of the genealogy of this male heir, Obed,

20. Ackerman, "Personal Is Political," 453.

21. This is so odd that some suspect that two different stories, one about Naomi and one about Ruth, were spliced together to form one story. See Athalya Brenner, "Naomi and Ruth," *Vetus Testamentum* 33, no. 4 (1983): 385–97.

who is said to be the forefather of David (Ruth 4:18–22). And it is David who, at the end of the book of Ruth, is the main focus. Indeed, "David" is the last word of this book.

Needless to say, the ending of Ruth is intriguing and confusing. In terms of love, given this ending, Ruth's contribution seems to be both simultaneously lauded and also diminished. As such, whether the mention of Ruth's love of Naomi comes from Ruth's higher position, as Ackerman argues, is unclear considering the uniqueness of the case, the indirectness of the assertion of her love, and the confusion over whether a foreign widow who has a child via Levirate marriage would indeed rank higher than a native Israelite widow. What is clear, however, are the ways in which Ruth embodies covenantal love insofar as she remains loyal and faithful to Naomi. As such, Ruth and her actions—indeed, her story—undoubtedly exemplify *hesed*, a term and concept related to *ahav*.[22]

In terms of the gendered nuances of love, however, the book of Ruth again evinces ambivalence. Considering that the end of the book moves away from Ruth in order to focus on Naomi and the rebirth of her family, it is unclear whether Ruth is indeed better than seven sons as the women joyously claim (Ruth 4:15). The ending seems to diminish Ruth's love and all her actions that exemplify it described in the preceding narrative. She is only important insofar as she is needed to bear a male child, one who will become the forefather of an important Israelite king. Hence, though out of all the female subjects of love Ruth is given the most positive outcome, perhaps because the object of her love is female, the ambivalent tone of the ending still suggests some underlying discomfort. Even if the object of love is the expected gender, even if the story centers on two females, even if the story ends with a woman being celebrated by other female characters, perhaps the writers or editors of the biblical text remain piqued that the subject of love was a female—a foreign female, even—and took steps to mitigate and lessen her centrality, especially her role as the one who loves. As such, they inserted the patrilineal genealogy that leads to David, the male character whose name means beloved, so as to override the love of his foreign ancestress, Ruth.

VICTIMS OF LOVE: DINAH AND TAMAR

From women as subjects of love, we now turn to the very opposite, women as victims, namely, the victims of rape. Considering that love seems completely

---

22. As I noted in the first chapter, *hesed* and other terms related to *ahav* are not discussed at length in this work.

out of place when discussing an act of sexual violence and, in particular, rape, our examination centers on why these disturbing stories of rape mention *ahav* at all.

The first story in Genesis 34 describes how Dinah, the daughter of Jacob and Leah, during her visit to the women of Canaan, meets Shechem, who is described as a leader or chief (*nasi'*) of the area (Gen. 34:2). When Shechem sees Dinah, the text states that he took or seized her, and laid down with her, and humbled, afflicted, or oppressed (*'anah*) her (Gen. 34:2). His violent action—one which the NRSV translates as "lay with her by force"—is oddly in conflict with what comes next. Genesis 34:3 states that Shechem's "soul [*nephesh*] was drawn to Dinah" and "he loved [*ahav*]" her, so much so that he demands that his father get permission from Dinah's parents for her to become his wife (v. 4).

The strange juxtaposition of violence and tenderness in Genesis 34:2–4, and especially the use of love in a story that concerns rape, has led some interpreters to argue that this story really concerns sexual relationships that lacked the approval of the proper authority figures, in this case, Dinah's parents.[23] Others try to make sense of the appearance of *ahav* in this story by arguing that *ahav* means lust, not love, as *ahav* is associated with sex and marriage.[24] In contrast to this line of thought, some maintain that the love language is probably genuine and that this was an attempt by Shechem to rectify the situation.[25]

Susan Ackerman, however, posits a different interpretation, arguing that the "seemingly discordant juxtaposition of rape and love is not necessarily so discordant after all" but rather "appropriate."[26] If *ahav* involves nuances of power—or, as she puts it, is "a term connoting dominance"—then it is only fitting that it is used to describe "a crime of domination."[27] As rape concerns power, that is, overpowering the victim and asserting the dominance of the perpetrator, and as *ahav* also has connotations of power because of its use in

23. Lyn M. Bechtel, "What If Dinah Is Not Raped? (Genesis 34)," *Journal for the Study of the Old Testament* 19, no. 62 (1994): 19–36; Tikva Frymer-Kensky, "Law and Philosophy: The Case of Sex in the Bible," *Semeia* 45 (1989): 89–102, esp. 95; Nick Wyatt, "The Story of Dinah and Shechem," *Ugarit-Forschungen* 22 (1991): 435–36.

24. Sharon Jeansonne, *The Women of Genesis: From Sarah to Potiphar's Wife* (Minneapolis: Augsburg Fortress Press, 1990), 91.

25. Meir Sternberg, *The Poetics of Biblical Narrative: Ideological Literature and the Drama of Reading* (Bloomington: Indiana University Press, 1985), 447; Dana Nolan Fewell and David M. Gunn, "Tipping the Balance: Sternberg's Reader and the Rape of Dinah," *Journal of Biblical Literature* 110, no. 2 (1991): 193–211 (197).

26. Ackerman, "Personal Is Political," 456.

27. Ackerman, "Personal is Political," 456.

treaties or covenants, so Ackerman argues that this is a fitting term to use in this story about rape.

She offers a similar explanation for the use of *ahav* in another story of rape, this time of David's daughter Tamar by her half-brother Amnon, the crown prince (2 Sam. 13). Unlike in the first story about Dinah, there is less confusion over whether Amnon's violation of his sister indeed constituted rape or merely entailed unauthorized premarital sexual relations. Amnon, who is said multiple times to love Tamar (2 Sam. 13:1, 4, 15), lures his half-sister into his bedroom by pretending to be sick. Once she is there, 2 Samuel 13:14 states that Amnon seized her, and humbled, afflicted, oppressed, or raped (*'anah*) her, and laid down with her. Though the same word is used both times for rape (*'anah*), the protest by Tamar to Amnon before the rape to ask their father, David, for permission to marry her instead of forcing himself on her (vv. 12–13), as well as her plea after the rape to refrain from sending her away without an offer of marriage (v. 16), more clearly stress the horror of Amnon's crime. Amnon, the crown prince and the son of the much-loved David, is clearly depraved, behaving even worse than the Canaanite rapist, Shechem.

Discordantly, again, *ahav* is used—multiple times—to describe Amnon's reaction to Tamar. In Amnon's case, however, the use of *ahav* mainly occurs before the rape (2 Sam. 13:1, 4), not after, as in the case of Shechem. In contrast to Shechem, the single instance of *ahav* after the rape describes his instant transformation (2 Sam. 13:15): after the rape, 2 Samuel 13:15 states that Amnon hated (*sana'*) Tamar with a great hatred (*sana'*), one which was bigger or greater than the love (*ahav*) with which he had loved (*ahav*) her. This leads him to kick her out of his room immediately after his crime without offering marriage as recourse (2 Sam. 13:15–16), a wrong that Tamar decries as even worse than the act he just perpetrated (v. 16). Amnon's actions and the hate that follows his love (or lust) will be matched by the hatred (*sana'*) of Tamar's full brother Absalom who will later kill his half-brother as payback for his crime (2 Sam. 13:23–39).

Again, according to Ackerman, though the two stories of rape describe something very different from love, *ahav* is an appropriate word to use because these tales concern power: two men of privilege overpower and abuse characters who are less powerful because of their gender. Ackerman's convincing conclusion about the power connotations of *ahav* compels us to dig deeper. If *ahav* is intertwined with power, whose power continues to be supported and privileged in and through these stories? And when we look closely at the aftermaths of the rapes, the point of these stories, in part, seems to be to assert male dominance and dominion over love and its power. As we will see, the stories of the rape of two women, Dinah and Tamar, affirm this idea by depicting men as the real victims of *ahav* and, therefore, as love's rightful avengers.

The aftermath of the rape of Dinah in Genesis 34 depicts the transformation of a violation of a woman into that of men. After the rape, Shechem's father, Hamor, comes to Dinah's father and brothers to request that they let Dinah become Shechem's wife (Gen. 34:8–12). Perhaps attempting to undo the egregious offense by his son, Hamor also suggests that the two groups intermarry and live with each other, that is, become kin (Gen. 34:8–10). Dinah's brothers deceptively tell Hamor that they cannot marry into a group where the men are uncircumcised. And when Hamor tells his people, the Shechemites, that the Israelites are rich, they agree to be circumcised as a prelude to intermarriage (Gen. 34:13–17). While the men of the town are indisposed, two of Dinah's brothers, Simeon and Levi, take the opportunity to kill all the men of the town and seize their women, children, and wealth (Gen. 34:25–31). They also retrieve Dinah, who is still being held at Hamor's house, and she is never heard from again in the Hebrew text.

A conversation between Jacob and his two sons after their destruction of the town reveals the characters' motivations (Gen. 34:30–31): "Then Jacob said to Simeon and Levi, 'You have brought trouble on me by making me odious to the inhabitants of the land . . . my numbers are few, and if they gather themselves against me and attack me, I shall be destroyed, both I and my household.' But they said, 'Should our sister be treated like a prostitute?'" It is clear from their conversation that the welfare of Dinah, the victim, is not the primary concern of either her father or her brothers.[28] Rather, Jacob's main focus is the possibility of retaliation by other Canaanites (Gen. 34:30), while that of the brothers is their right to obtain compensation for the damage done to their sister's reputation and value, which has been degraded to those of a prostitute. That the brothers' brutal payback, which consists of theft, pillaging, and murder, might have been motivated by and likely led to the enrichment of the family, especially the brothers, is never mentioned.[29]

This disregard for Dinah continues throughout the narrative. Dinah, for all the violence done to her and in her name, is never given a chance to speak

---

28. Both Jacob and his sons also seem generally undisturbed by the excessiveness of the brutality whereby an entire town has been destroyed, its male denizens murdered, and its women and children enslaved, likely making them vulnerable to sexual abuse. On this, see Carolyn Pressler, "Wives and Daughters, Bond and Free: Views of Women in the Slave Laws of Exodus 21.2–11," in *Gender and Law in the Hebrew Bible and the Ancient Near East*, ed. Victory H. Matthews, Bernard M. Levinson, and Tikva Frymer-Kensky (Sheffield: Sheffield Academic, 1998), 155.

29. The story seems to center around *ahav* and its connection to the appetites of men, especially unsavory ones such as greed and lust: Shechem, in raping Dinah, and Dinah's brothers in destroying Shechem, takes for themselves what they desire. Moreover, both the Israelite and the Shechemites are motivated by greed: The Shechemites are convinced by Hamor to intermarry with the Israelites in order to obtain part of their wealth (Gen. 34:21–24), while the destruction of Shechem leads Jacob's family to obtain loot.

in the story. She is also never heard from again in the biblical text.[30] Rather, she is treated—not as a victim—but as stolen or damaged goods and is quickly sidelined in the story so that the supposed "real" victims can be given airtime instead. The troubling depiction or, more accurately, lack of concern for Dinah clearly shows that, in the text, it is the men related to Dinah who are the real victims of love. It is therefore the right of these men to avenge love's violation.

The text seems to double down on this disturbing conclusion by subtly supporting and condoning the actions of Dinah's brothers. The marriage, which Shechem offers after the rape of Dinah, would have led to intermarriage, kinship ties, and covenants between the Shechemites, who are Canaanites, and the Israelites.[31] However, intermarriage to the Canaanites is imagined as the worst thing possible in other parts of the Hebrew corpus: A direct contravention of God's instruction (Exod. 23:20–33; 34:11–16; Josh. 23:11–13; 1 Kgs. 11), it was a betrayal of Israel's covenant with YHWH.[32] So great was the threat posed by intermarriage that the Israelites were even commanded to annihilate the Canaanites so as to eliminate this peril (Exod. 23:20–33; 34:11–16; Deut. 7:1–4).[33] In light of this background, the brothers' actions are not deplorable but commendable. Acting on behalf of the real victims of Shechem's abuse—their God, their patriarchal family, and their future covenant—their punishment of the Canaanites, according to the biblical text, fits their crime.

Male dominance and authority over love is similarly asserted in the story of the rape of Tamar. The silencing and sidelining of Tamar occur in the immediate aftermath of her rape when she decries her abuse:[34] "But Tamar

30. In contrast to the biblical account, in some postbiblical traditions, such as the *Targum of Job*, the *Liber antiquitatum biblicarum* of Pseudo-Philo, and the *Testament of Job*, Dinah is said to have married Job.

31. This story emphasizes covenants by naming the father of Shechem as Hamor, which means "donkey," an animal frequently used to make a covenant. See Nahum Sarna, *Genesis = Be-reshit: The traditional Hebrew Text with the New JPS Translation* (Philadelphia: Jewish Publication Society, 1989), 233.

32. *Ahav*'s connection with sex, family, covenant, election, and therefore similarity and difference in this story explains the use of circumcision as a means of deception. Circumcision not only entails the physical change of the "part of the body used by Shechem in his violent passion" (Sarna, *Genesis = Be-reshit*, 360) and therefore is linked to sex, family, and reproduction, but it is also the marker of the covenant, one which symbolizes the regeneration, reproduction, and continuance of the family of Abraham (Gen. 17). As such, the use of circumcision in this story again connects *ahav* to family, Israel's election promises, and its covenant with God.

33. Because Israelite identity centers on its antithesis or difference to the Canaanites, who are imagined as "the other," intermarriage, especially with the Canaanites, was seen as a source of threat to the very self-understanding and conceptualization—the identity—of Israel.

34. Unlike Dinah, Tamar, perhaps because she is royalty, does not remain silent about her abuse. There are other differences between the two figures as well. The narrative about

put ashes on her head and tore the long robe that she was wearing; she put her hand on her head and went away, crying aloud as she went. Her brother Absalom said to her, 'Has Amnon your brother been with you? Be quiet for now, my sister; he is your brother; do not take this to heart.' So Tamar remained, a desolate woman, in her brother Absalom's house" (2 Sam. 13:19–20).

We find out later in the text that Absalom hushes his sister not only to mollify her but to lay the groundwork for revenge. Two years after the rape, Absalom, Tamar's full brother, plans a family gathering and, when the guests are inebriated, has his servants murder Amnon (2 Sam. 13:23–39). Considering the despicable depiction of Amnon, the rapist, and the tragic portrayal of Tamar, it is easy to sympathize with, if not even applaud, Absalom's action. Who wouldn't resonate with the angry and aggrieved Absalom? He even names one of his daughters after his poor sister Tamar, almost in memoriam, showing the deep effects of the rape (1 Sam. 14:27).

A closer look at the narrative, however, reveals the complicated motivations and feelings behind Absalom's murder of his brother. Considering that Tamar, like Dinah, is never consulted about her wishes, and considering her tragic fate whereby she never marries and remains "a desolate woman," this act of revenge by Absalom neither takes her feelings into account nor ultimately improves her life. The act of revenge therefore is not just for her sake, but as much, if not more, for his sake as her male avenger. Indeed, Absalom has an additional incentive, aside from payback, for doing away with his disturbed older half-brother, Amnon. As the third (or possibly second, as the text never speaks of David's second son) in line for the throne (1 Chr. 3:2), Absalom, in killing Amnon, who is the crown prince, not only punishes his sister's rapist but also eliminates a rival for the throne. That Absalom has political ambitions is clear as he later nearly successfully tries to usurp the throne of his father, David (2 Sam. 15). Considering that Absalom has much to gain by getting rid of Amnon, it is difficult to discern whether his murder is purely out of concern for his sister or motivated by these other desires.

What the complicated motives of the male avengers reveal, especially when considered alongside the sideling of the actual female victims, are the priorities of the narratives. The rape of Tamar, like that of Dinah, is simply an inciting incident for the more important melodrama involving the male characters. Tamar's story and rape, succinctly told in one chapter (2 Sam. 13), is only of concern insofar as it leads to Absalom's revenge against his half-brother and,

---

the rape of Dinah involves going too far outside the family, that is, intermarriage to a banned outsider group, the Canaanites. In contrast, the story about the rape of Tamar entails the opposite—getting too close within the family via an incestuous sexual relationship. One is too different or too far; the other, too similar or too close. In both cases, however, their abuses lead to acts of vengeance by male members of their family.

later, against his unresponsive and irresponsible father—a story that fills several chapters (2 Sam. 13–19). More salient to our purposes, by depicting Absalom employing violence in order to avenge his sister, Tamar, this story again transforms an act of violence against a woman—one done in the name of love—primarily into a violation against a man. As it is the power of men that are undermined by violations of *ahav*, it is therefore their right to take actions, even those that are deplorable and excessive, in order to reclaim it. Love, both the violations and vindications done in its name, are therefore asserted once again as within the purview of men.

Even God, who is imagined as a male deity in the Hebrew text, appears to view and treat love similarly. The upheavals in David's family—the "love" and rape of Tamar, which leads to the murder of Amnon by Absalom, and Absalom's rebellion against his father, David—are all said to be part of God's punishment of David for his adultery with Bathsheba and the murder of her husband, Uriah (2 Sam. 11). Hence, the calamity that befalls the house of David itself stems from divine comeuppance for David's abuses of power and his lack of self-control—i.e., his desire for a married woman. Hence, YHWH, a male deity, avenges David's possible rape of Bathsheba (as it is unclear how much power she had to refuse the king's sexual advances), an offense against both God and Uriah, her husband, by letting David's daughter, Tamar, be raped in kind. According to the text, women, and the suffering and violence done to them, are therefore mere tools used by men to punish and avenge each other. In such a scenario, the wrong done to a woman, illogically, is not mainly or ultimately a wrong done to her, but to the man or men responsible for her.

These disturbing stories about the rape of Dinah and Tamar further reveal the gendered notions of *ahav*. As noted in my discussion, women who assert an active role in love are playing a dangerous game: Rebekah and Michal suffer a disastrous end. Ruth is the exception, perhaps because the object of her love is another female. Even she, however, is dismissed or ignored at the end of the story. Conversely, the stories about Dinah and Tamar show that things do not turn out better if you are the female object of love. Instead, sometimes they turn out much worse. And the fact that you cannot win in love as a woman, either as its object or subject, suggests that *ahav* might have a particular gendered nuance in the Hebrew Bible. That is, women in the Hebrew text might be more closely tied to the negative aspects of love.[35]

---

35. When parents love children, especially male children, it also is usually said to lead to suffering, separation, sacrifice, or some other tragic result. Cf., Abraham of Isaac (Gen. 22:2), Isaac and Rebekah of Esau and Jacob (Gen. 25:28), and Jacob of Joseph (Gen. 37:3, 4) and of Benjamin (Gen. 44:20). It may be that the women, as they are the ones who bear these important sons, taint them in some manner, imbuing their love with love's negative ramifications.

Considering the terrible things that befall women who have the misfortune to be connected to *ahav* in some manner, it seems that, when it comes to love, female characters are targeted for special punishment and retaliation. This suspicion is supported by other accounts of love in the Hebrew corpus. As I stated, it is usually male characters who are said to love female characters in the biblical text. And unlike Amnon and Shechem, some male characters do love female characters without recourse to violence or abuse: Isaac is said to love Rebekah (Gen. 24:67); Jacob is said to love Rachel (Gen. 29:18, 20, 30); Samson is said to love Delilah (Judg. 16:4, 15); Elkanah is said to love Hannah, the mother of Samuel (1 Sam. 1:5); Solomon is said to love his many foreign wives (1 Kgs. 11:1–2); Rehoboam is said to love his wife Maacah, the daughter of Absalom (2 Chr. 11:21); and Ahasuerus is said to love Esther (Esth. 2:17).

However, even in these less violent descriptions of love, what is striking is the negative portrayals of these supposedly beloved women. Barring a few cases, such as Rehoboam and Elkanah, in all other instances where a male character is said to love a female character, the woman is depicted as deceptive, manipulating, or in some way taking advantage of the loving man.[36] This points to something of a paradox, albeit one that again paints women in a bad light. Love, according to the text, is simultaneously both the purview of men and yet something women wield and manipulate, often more proficiently than men, for their own nefarious purposes. As a result, women's particular talents in love leave men weak and vulnerable. As we saw with Tamar, love can even be a kind of affliction that makes men do crazy and foolish things, leading them both to violate women and to attack these violators in turn. Thus, the logic behind the targeting of female characters who are loved or love is revealed: As love, especially its abuses or negative fallout, is largely the fault of women, it is only fair that women should bear the bulk of the punishment.

Two contradictory understandings of love and women, hence, are present in the Hebrew text. The first is that women are simultaneously powerless objects when it comes to love, easily violated and damaged by men, and therefore in need of protection and vengeance when necessary. Hence, when women are attacked, it's their male relatives who are the real victims. In contrast, there is a second idea: Women are especially wily in love, and therefore quite powerful in this regard, able to tempt and lure men into violent and damaging behavior. Hence, women can use love's great power and potential for pain to victimize men. In either case, it is men who are the real victims of

---

36. Though the story of Jacob and his paramour, Rachel, might seem like an outlier, her story also involves duplicity and deception: Rachel, who is loved by Jacob, never tells him of her theft of her father's teraphim and as a result leads to Jacob's inadvertent curse on the thief (Gen. 31:32). Moreover, her marriage to Jacob is also the result of duplicity, as Jacob is duped to first marry Leah instead of Rachel, as promised (Gen. 29:16–30).

love; and women, as the perpetuators of this damage, should be held responsible and punished for this violation.

These conflicting ideas speak to why the biblical text, which was written and edited by men, seem opposed to women being associated with love and react to their connection with blame, abuse, and erasure. Love and women, according to these writers, are a dangerous mix, capable of causing chaos, division, and even death for men. As we will see in the next section, there might be an additional reason for this feeling of threat and insecurity: Love, because of its connection to sex and fertility, is quite often associated with women. As a result, love is easily imagined as a kind of feminine ability and power—one which, as I argued in previous chapters, is a divine force powerful enough to influence or sway even God.

THE CULMINATION OF LOVE: THE SONG OF SONGS

The most dramatic display of these contradictory feelings about women and love is found in the Song of Songs, also known as the Song of Solomon, or Canticle of Canticles. The Song of Songs is one of the central books about love in the Hebrew text, especially erotic or sexual love. According to one scholar, it is the "only text in the Hebrew Bible in which sex, desire, love, and romance can all be found."[37] Sex, though the Hebrew text seems generally reticent on this point, is depicted as an indirect component of love in many Hebrew tales. Stories about Isaac and Rebekah (Gen. 24:67), Jacob and Rachel (Gen. 29:18), Hannah and Elkanah (1 Sam. 1), and Michal and David (1 Sam. 18, 20) mention both love (*ahav*) and children, the result of sex (or in the case of Michal, the deliberate lack of children), showing that sex is indeed a part of love. However, it is only in the Song of Songs that the erotic and sexual aspects of love receive focused attention, being lavishly described and even celebrated. That the Song of Songs is the only book where this natural connection between sex and love is fully acknowledged suggests a deliberate suppression of this link.

Before exploring this possible suppression more closely, a brief overview of the book will help to orient our discussion. Fittingly, the name of the book of Song of Songs speaks to its content and form. The name, which comes from the first two words of the book (*shir ha-shirim*), in Hebrew connotes the superlative. As such, the name according to the first two words of the book suggests that it consists of the best or the ultimate song ever composed. And

37. J. Cheryl Exum, "Desire, Love, and Romance in the Hebrew Bible," *Oxford Research Encyclopedia of Religion*, https://doi.org/10.1093/acrefore/9780199340378.013.54.

unsurprisingly, as now so also in ancient times the best or ultimate song or poem would naturally be about—what else?—love, especially erotic and amorous love. Indeed, what better way of language to talk about or understand love—perhaps the best or maybe only way to talk about or understand love— than in lyric, poetic, or musical form? In terms of content, as the "only true romance in the Hebrew Bible,"[38] the Song of Songs mentions love or *ahav* quite a bit and gives Deuteronomy a run for its money. Moreover, speaking to the centrality of love in this book, the Song of Songs also has the "densest concentration of love language" in the Hebrew text, with *ahav* used eighteen times in 117 verses.[39]

As expected of the greatest love song, there are many issues and concerns surrounding this book. For the sake of space, however, most of the questions about the Song of Songs have to be largely put aside.[40] Instead, for our purposes, I will focus on one key aspect of the book: gender and the ways it impacts and interacts with love. In so doing, I argue that this work both celebrates the connection between women and love, especially erotic love, and also expresses anxiety of it. Fearful that women might possess the power of love and be better able to wield it, the male editors and writers of the text push back and retaliate in and through the text. What we see in the Song of Songs, therefore, is both an acknowledgment of this connection between love and women, and also simultaneously an undermining of and recoiling from this idea.

As interpreters have frequently noted, one of the notable aspects of the Song of Songs is that it somehow became part of the canon despite the book never mentioning God (at least, not directly) or indeed anything particularly religious.[41] Rather, as I mentioned earlier, the book is a discourse on love, especially erotic aspects of love, which is presented in poetic form—or as Longman puts it, the Song of Songs constitutes "something like an erotic psalter."[42] More broadly, the book consists of a loose and sometimes confusing dialogue of sorts, that may or may not be cohesive, between two unnamed characters, one female—who is sometimes referred to as the Shulammite—and

38. Exum, "Desire, Love, and Romance," n.p.

39. Aren M. Wilson-Wright, "Love Conquers All: Song of Songs 8:6b–7a as a Reflex of the Northwest Semitic Combat Myth," *Journal of Biblical Literature* 134, no. 2 (2015): 333–45 (343).

40. An overview of issues about the Song of Songs, such as dating, authorship, genre, history of interpretation, canonicity, coherence, poetics, structure, voice, and relationship to other kinds of Near/Middle Eastern love poems and lyrics can be found in Tremper Longman III, *The Song of Songs* (Grand Rapids: Eerdmans, 2001).

41. Gianni Barbiero, *Song of Songs: A Close Reading* (Leiden/Boston: Brill, 2011), esp. 464–66. Later, the Songs will be read allegorically as the love between God and Israel, or God and the church. See, e.g., Jonathan Kaplan and Aren M. Wilson-Wright, "How the Song of Songs Became a Divine Love Song," *Biblical Interpretation* 26 (2018): 334–51; Michael Fishbane, *The JPS Commentary: Song of Songs* (Philadelphia: Jewish Publication Society, 2015), xix–xxiv.

42. Longman, *The Song of Songs*, 14.

the other male. In this dialogue, they express their erotic longings for each other in heightened language, mainly to each other. The woman, at times, also tells of her longings for the man to a group of women called the "daughters of Jerusalem."

Though the Songs of Songs is a dialogue, the centrality of the female character sets it apart from other books in the Hebrew corpus. That is, though there is an unnamed male figure who also speaks and replies in the book, and who is given only slightly less than half the lines in the work, it is unusual that the Songs of Songs sustains attention to and gives space to the *female* protagonist. It is her words that begin the book, and it is her voice, her sentiments, and her feelings, especially her frank statements about her desire for and pursuit of the man, that remain the most prominent and memorable aspects of the work. Even in books that focus on women characters, such as Ruth and Esther, the readers largely get little to no access into the thoughts, feelings, and emotions of these female characters. Apart from the Song of Songs, we never hear a story from the woman's perspective, especially not about her sexual desires.

Therefore, in terms of love, the Song of Songs is one of a kind. It is the only book in the Hebrew text that runs counter to the prevalent pattern whereby men are predominantly the ones who do the loving, that is, are the subjects of love. With the Songs of Songs, we have an entire book where the more prominent *subject* of love—the more prominent dialogue partner—is female! This book, more than any other in the Hebrew corpus, therefore, seems to acknowledge the seemingly obvious notion that women can be central and active in love, and not merely a supporting player in stories about men's love. As a result, this book has received much attention from scholars of the Bible, especially feminist scholars, many of whom view the work as a counter to the more misogynistic texts in the Hebrew corpus, a book where "femaleness and femininity reign supreme."[43] Indeed, as J. Cheryl Exum notes, this text "arouses our desire," especially those of female readers who very much "want to have an ancient book that celebrates woman's sexuality and whose

43. Athalya Brenner, *A Feminist Companion to the Song of Songs* (Sheffield: Sheffield Academic, 1993); Athalya Brenner and Carole R. Fontaine, eds., *The Song of Songs: A Feminist Companion to the Bible* (Sheffield: Sheffield Academic, 2000); Phyllis Trible, *God and the Rhetoric of Sexuality* (Philadelphia: Fortress, 1978). Fokkelien van Dijk-Hemmnes, "The Imagination of Power and the Power of Imagination: An Intertextual Analysis of Two Biblical Love Songs: The Songs of Songs and Hosea 2," *Journal for the Study of the Old Testament* 44 (1989): 75–88; Athalya Brenner, "To See Is to Assume: Whose Love Is Celebrated in the Song of Songs?," *Biblical Interpretation* 1, no. 3 (1993): 265–84 (273). Brenner writes, "It can hardly be denied that femaleness and femininity reign supreme in it [the Song]. . . . Female figurations are the dominant actors in the Song: they are strong, articulate, outspoken, active; in fact, much more so than their male counterparts. . . . There is no equality of the sexes in the Song. . . . There is female superiority" ("To See," 273).

protagonist is an active, desiring, autonomous subject."[44] Considering the personal stakes, it is easy to see why many interpreters view the Song as a generally positive, "gynocentric, egalitarian, and nonstereotypical celebration of human sexual love."[45]

Though the desire to view this book as a nonsexist celebration of women and their sexuality is understandable, when we dig a bit deeper, however, things get more complicated. On the one hand, this book finally acknowledges, perhaps even celebrates, the natural connection between women and love, especially erotic love, by centrally featuring a female protagonist. On the other, the way that the book goes about this and what the text does to this female protagonist again speak to more ambivalent and disturbing feelings by the male authors and editors of this work. To be sure, we should acknowledge that, despite some arguments otherwise, it is likely that the authors and editors of the Song of Songs were men.[46] Though we know little else about these authors or editors, when we consider their likely gender in light of the centrality of the female protagonist, especially her eroticism and expressions of female sexual longing, the book takes on an ickier tone. Like in many artworks and movies, the female character of the Song of Songs is largely a male construct, a "fetching ventriloquy"—the object of the male gaze. These characters in the Song of Songs are "not real women—but women as imagined by men," and as written by men in order "to meet the desires and needs of other Israelite men."[47]

If the female character of the Song of Songs is largely the construction of men, can we really say that she is the subject of love? Rather, as a product of male authors, she, despite being the purported subject, remains largely the object. Indeed, she is doubly the object as she is both an object of love of the male authors who created and imagined her and also of the unnamed male lover of the text. As the ostensible subject but also the object of love, the female protagonist becomes liminal and ambivalent, neither one thing or another. This in-between, nonbinary state of the female protagonist, as I will discuss

44. J. Cheryl Exum "Ten Things Every Feminist Should Know about the Song of Songs," in *The Song of Songs: A Feminist Companion to the Bible,* ed. Athalya Brenner (Sheffield: Sheffield Academic, 2000), 24–35 (26).

45. Kathryn Imray, "Love Is (Strong as) Death: Reading the Song of Songs through Proverbs 1–9," *Catholic Biblical Quarterly* 75, no. 4 (2013): 649–96 (650).

46. On the possible female authorship, see Athalya Brenner, *The Israelite Woman: Social Role and Literary Type in Biblical Narrative* (Sheffield: JSOT Press, 1985), 46–56; Roland E. Murphy, *The Song of Songs: A Commentary on the Book of Canticles or the Song of Songs,* Hermeneia (Minneapolis: Fortress, 1990), 70.

47. David J. A. Clines, "Why Is There a Song of Songs, and What Does It Do to You If You Read It?," in *Interested Parties: The Ideology of Writers and Readers* (Sheffield: Sheffield Phoenix, 2009), 94–121 (99, 104–5).

shortly, affects and influences the way that love, especially erotic love, is portrayed and understood in this book.

This confusion over the role of the woman as both subject and object, moreover, explains why the erotic and sexual aspects of the work can both feel celebratory and worshipful, and also simultaneously pornographic and voyeuristic.[48] Take for example Song 7, which follows an Arabic poetic form known as the *wasf*, whereby each part of the lover's body is detailed and praised. In the second-person (you), the male protagonist in Song 7 describes the beauty of the female lover, from her feet to her head, using images and metaphors from nature. While there are similar poems and descriptions of the male body in the book, such as Song 5:10–16, they are in the third-person (he) and, as such, at a remove. Moreover, some argue the description of the parts of the male body are less stimulating and sensuous. As such, the female body, much more than that of the man, seems to be thoroughly unveiled and put on display. Yet the intent of this viewing, this extended textual cataloguing, is left ambiguous. Is it worshipful and adoring? Or is it leering, a kind of "checking out" of the female body, which "begins with her feet and proceeds upwards, including her apparently exposed genital area"?[49]

This confusion explains the strange and discomfiting sense of unease and danger that lingers throughout the Song of Songs—a feeling that the adoration can turn suddenly into something more dangerous and threatening. Take, for example, the ardent description of the female physical form in Song 7: On the one hand, the description seems passionate and stimulating, albeit a bit odd (e.g., "your belly is a heap of wheat" [7:2], "your breasts are like two fawns" [7:3]). On the other hand, however, not only is the female body exposed and displayed but it is also discussed in a way that renders it fragmented or even cut up. The woman portrayed in the work is "not a complete woman, but a collocation of body parts: a tower-like neck, a belly like a heap of wheat, breasts like two fawns, eyes like pools, a tower-like nose."[50] What is the intent of this fragmentation? Is this the adoring gaze of a lover or something out of a violent horror or slasher film where the body of the female is dismembered, with each piece lovingly fawned over by the sociopath? Whatever the intent, the outcome of the cataloging of body parts has the effect of dehumanization that verges on violence.

It is difficult not to feel a sense of violence and, therefore, threat with this textual fragmentation of the female form. Tellingly, this threat is not just imagined but actuated in the poem. In a strange and disturbing sequence,

48. Clines, "Why Is There a Song of Songs, 120.
49. Donald C. Polaski, "What Will Ye See in the Shulammite? Women, Power and Panopticism in the Song of Songs," *Biblical Interpretation* 5, no. 1 (1997): 64–81 (72).
50. Exum, "Ten Things," 33.

Song 5 describes how the female lover, while looking for her beloved, meets guards who forcibly expose, beat, and abuse her: "Making their rounds in the city the sentinels found me; they beat me, they wounded me, they took away my mantle, those sentinels of the walls" (Song 5:7). Though this sudden and confusing act of violence (some even argue gang rape)[51] in Song 5 is often ignored or dismissed as a dream, the threat and the message underlying the threat are real: *"bad things happen to sexually active, forward women"* (italics original).[52]

This sense of threat hints of an unease and ambivalence about women, especially their sexuality, and with it, a desire to mitigate and control its power and expression. The violent interlude with the guards (Song 5:7); the negative appraisals of the female protagonist's sexuality as immature (8:8–9); her similarities to the "bad woman," the strange temptress of Proverbs 1–9;[53] the mention of her brothers ("sons of my mother") who are angry at her for not keeping her "own vineyard" (Song 1:6), and who want to guard her ("If she is a wall, we will build upon her a battlement . . . if she is a door, we will enclose her with boards of cedar" [Song 8:9]); the emphasis on her inaccessibility through her depiction as a walled garden (4:12; 8:8–9), a bird hiding on a cliff (2:14), a guarded tower (4:4; 7:5), or a woman inside her house watching from a lattice window (2:9)—all of this speaks to a desire to control the woman, especially her body, erotic longings, and expression. And through this control, suppress and control the power and manifestation of her love. And so, strangely, the Song of Songs seems to both celebrate women and their sexuality and also to express a desire to keep women locked up and under control.

This desire for control stems, it seems, from a fear of women, especially their love, which is portrayed as having the power and ability to weaken, debilitate, and subdue men. The martial images and militaristic metaphors found throughout the book reflect this anxiety. Not only is love likened to war in the Song of Songs, but the book also portrays the woman and her love as a source of terrible chaos and destruction.[54] Song 1:9, for example, likens the woman to a mare, probably in heat, who has the power to disturb the male stallions, and hence, to upturn the chariots and the cavalry.[55] So also Song 6:10 likens the woman to an army—and therefore the violence and destruction it causes—by describing the woman's beauty as "terrible as an

51. Renita J. Weems, "Song of Songs," in *The New Interpreter's Bible*, ed. Leander E. Keck (Nashville: Abingdon, 2001), 5:361–434 (412).

52. Exum "Ten Things," 30.

53. Imray, "Love Is (Strong as) Death," 649–65.

54. The parallel to war is found in other literature. See Danilo Verde, *Conquered Conquerors: Love and War in the Song of Songs* (Atlanta: SBL Press, 2020), 4. Verde argues that "love is war" is one of the main ideas of the Song of Songs (*Conquered Conquerors*, 4).

55. Imray, "Love Is (Strong as) Death," 655–56.

army with banners." Like the resplendent banner and army, she is beautiful and awe-inspiring, but in her beauty lies the power to ruin and destroy men. No wonder the male narrator begs her to "turn away your eyes from me, for they overwhelm me!" (6:5).[56]

CONCLUSION

In the Song of Songs, as in the stories discussed in previous chapters, love is frequently tied to violence, war, and death. Women are often at the bad ends of this connection as objects and/or victims. Even when they are initially portrayed as active subjects, women are often recast as passive victims as the story progresses. At the same time, as shown by the Song of Songs, an acknowledgment and perhaps even a celebration of sexuality, and female sexuality in particular, are not wholly lacking in the Hebrew text. In this, the Hebrew text seems to evince a deep sense of ambivalence and confusion about women and their powers of love.

The reason for this ambivalence is understandable: The power of love, as we have seen, is immense, capable of influencing or swaying even God himself. Indeed, as I have discussed, love is so powerful and its potential for pain so great that it becomes a sort of divine presence. This raises a troubling problem: As love can have such a profound effect on God, love might be said to be equal to or even greater than God. This is especially problematic to the ancient authors given that women are shown to be more likely to possess this power and better capable of wielding it. Love, and its proximity to the feminine, can easily be imagined as a goddess—one that is perpetually absent *and* present in the Hebrew text; and one that exists in symbiotic opposition to God the Father.[57] The Hebrew text never says any of this aloud, instead forcing us to decipher the motivations through what is present as well as what is absent.

As I have tried to show throughout this chapter, the biblical imagination of love and women is beset by paradox. The alignment of females and love, especially erotic love, is viewed uncomfortably—perhaps even as intolerable by the biblical authors. In the Song of Songs, these mixed feelings are reflected through the problematic depiction of the unnamed female lover: the woman is alluring but terrifying; immensely powerful, but vulnerable to abuse; free in her expressions and, at points, in her movements, but also bounded and constrained by society and her male relatives. Women are even chastised and

---

56. Imray, "Love Is (Strong as) Death," 655.

57. On the missing goddess, especially in the creation story, see Ilona Rashkow, *Taboo or Not Taboo: Sexuality and Family in the Hebrew Bible* (Minneapolis: Fortress Press, 2000), 43–74.

punished, metaphorically and literally, for their desires. No wonder the female protagonist of the Song of Songs dances between being the subject and the object of love. Embedded in this waffling is a deep sense of confusion and uncertainty about the woman and about love.

Conclusion

The Question of Love

OVERVIEW

Love, or *ahav*, in the Hebrew Bible is envisioned as a great and mysterious force that often troubles and distorts the characters it touches, raising some to magnificent heights, but also eliciting the depravity of the guilty, and in many cases punishing the innocent. As such, the selection of stories that we have explored, understandably, exhibit mixed feelings about love. Divine, powerful, painful, and—as the text grudgingly and subtly accedes—perhaps more closely associated with women, love in these Hebrew tales is portrayed as an awesome yet ambivalent power. It, like a god, has the ability to create and destroy, to facilitate life or to hasten death. As we saw, the winners in love, such as David and Jacob, accrue riches, power, and lineage. In contrast, the losers of love, such as Saul, Jonathan, Michal, and most female characters associated with love, suffer indescribable loss. Most importantly, love, like a strange, strong affliction, is depicted as capable of taking hold of anyone, including God, twisting and affecting their character in troubling ways. Love, therefore, is shown to be a divine power of boundless pull and influence, one perhaps equal or maybe even greater than God.

SUMMARY OF CHAPTERS

Despite the false claim that the Hebrew Bible lacks love, I have found the opposite to be true.[1] The book is a limited study precisely because there is so much love in the Hebrew text. And while I have tried to keep this book to a manageable (and readable) size, there is certainly more love to go around and more ground yet to cover. Yet as a result of the scope of this topic, I have only explored a handful of stories that mention or feature love. There are many more stories about love in the Hebrew Scriptures that still require a prolonged exploration and thoughtful engagement.[2]

The first chapter laid the foundation for the exploration of love by summarizing the history of the study of love in the Hebrew Bible. Of particular note was the contribution of William Moran, who revealed the centrality of the covenant to the understanding of love in the Hebrew Scriptures. While Moran's conclusions have been reassessed and modified by recent interpreters, his central idea remains foundational. Indeed, the presence of different valences of love—theological, political, familial, and emotional—in the stories we have examined largely builds on the presence of love, *ahav*, in the descriptions of the covenant between Israel and God. Hence, the meaning of love as used and understood in covenants—that is, covenantal love—lingers throughout the Hebrew corpus, influencing and coloring how *ahav* is understood within it.

One of the key aspects of love as exemplified in the covenant is the focus on God's relationship with a particular group of people, especially the key family that comes to embody the nation of Israel in miniature. The second chapter revealed the importance of this divine relationship to an understanding of love by examining the oddly oppositional love preferences of the parents, Isaac and Rebekah, of their twins, Esau and Jacob. The oppositional love of the parents differentiates love into two kinds or types, contrasting a higher and holy love with a baser, appetite-driven, body-centric love. The contrast is used to assert the superiority and divinity of this higher love and also to question God and God's relationship to this love. While claiming the higher love as divine and superior, the story also undermines this claim by showing how this love leads to dubious actions and negative effects, such as discord, separation, and the disintegration of the family. Love, therefore, is depicted as divine and closely related to God, and also as a source of suffering and struggle.

---

1. On false claims that the Hebrew Bible lacks love, see Leon Morris, *Testaments of Love: A Study of Love in the Bible* (Grand Rapids: Eerdmans, 1981), 4.
2. For a disturbing look at divine love in the Prophets, see Renita J. Weems, *Battered Love: Marriage, Sex, and Violence in the Hebrew Prophets* (Minneapolis: Fortress, 1995). For love, especially of the neighbor, in ancient Jewish texts, see Kengo Akiayama, *The Love of Neighbour in Ancient Judaism: The Reception of Leviticus 19:18 in the Hebrew Bible, the Septuagint, the Book of Jubilees, the Dead Sea Scrolls, and the New Testament* (Leiden: Brill, 2018).

The aforementioned negative effects of love were highlighted in the third chapter of this book, which focused on the story of the first two kings of Israel, Saul and David, and the love relationship between them. Through the contrasting depictions of Saul and David, the text shows the power of love as well as its connection to the capricious preferences of God. While the divine favoritism and selection of David leads to love and, in turn, to success and political power, the divine rejection of Saul leads to the very opposite: the lack of love, failure, loss of power, and finally, death. Though the text never spells out the reasons behind God's inconsistent preferences, preferences which induce or reduce the love that comes from others, there are clues that suggest that God's rejection of Saul is due to God's own heartache and unrequited love. As such, the story of David and Saul reveals that God, like mortals, is also vulnerable to love and its effects, and in so doing, emphasizes love's tremendous power.

The story of the love relationship between David and Saul's firstborn son, Jonathan, the subject of chapter 4, underscored the power and mystery of love and, relatedly, of God's preference by outlining love's painful effects. Saul's rejection by God, and David's oppositional selection by God, influence and affect the behavior of others, especially those closest to David and Saul. The children of Saul, especially Jonathan, are particularly affected. The talented and promising firstborn son of Saul is said multiple times to love David, so much so that he even sides with him against his own father. Though interpreters have long wondered whether Jonathan and David's relationship was erotic or romantic, the text deliberately leaves the status of their one-sided love relationship unclear. This ambiguity, which is depicted as an effect of divine rejection, obscures the role that David had in fomenting intrafamilial discord and betrayal, which in turn aided David's usurpation of Saul's throne. The depiction of God as supportive of David's ruthless manipulations of the love of Jonathan and Saul once again portrays God as vulnerable to love's mysterious sway. Also enamored of the charismatic David, God allows his favorite to use the love he receives to cause tremendous pain and suffering.

The negative aspects of love receive more attention in the final chapter, which focused on certain female characters who are connected to love in the Hebrew text. Reflecting a level of discomfort with women as lovers, the narrative undermines, silences, and punishes women who are associated with love, be they the rare active subjects of love or the abject victims of male characters who are said to love them. This extreme reaction results from the recognition and fear of women's supposed powers with and of love. Fearful that women are better able to wield love and its tremendous power to weaken and harm men, the text undermines and punishes female characters who are associated with love in any way.

The clearest evidence of these mixed feelings about women and love is found in the Song of Songs. This book, which is envisioned by many as the culmination of the discussion of love, and as the most transcendent statement on love in the biblical corpus, closely links women with love, especially its awesome power. The Song of Songs tellingly both celebrates love, especially female expressions and desires for it, and also expresses fears of the power of love, especially as wielded and aligned with women. As such, at the end, love is portrayed ambivalently: as a divine, powerful, painful, mysterious, and ultimately feminine force.

FROM THE COVENANT TO THE CANTICLES

Considering that the Song of Songs or Canticles is considered by many to be the apotheosis of the discussion of love in the Hebrew text, it is fitting that we conclude this work by looking at its most famous passage on love. Not only does this book offer the most detailed portrait of love in the Hebrew Scriptures, but it has long been read allegorically as reflective of the ultimate love story, the one at the heart of the Hebrew Scriptures—the love relationship between God and Israel.[3] Some have even argued that the narrative arc of this romance, one which details the devastating highs and lows of love between God and Israel, should be traced from its origins in the covenant (or even earlier, in Eden) to its ultimate celebration in the Canticles.[4]

Indeed, the Song of Songs, with all of its ambivalent acknowledgment and terror of female love, can be viewed as a counterpart and countercharge to the masculine love asserted in the narratives of the covenant. After all, the god who demands that Israel love him in these narratives is imagined as a male suzerain or emperor. Therefore, the love in the covenant can be classified as a masculine kind of love—something that males, especially kings, directly demand from their underlings because they have the power to do so. Rebutting this claim is the voice and vision of love as conveyed in the Song of Songs and embodied by its female protagonist. This figure embodies both the feminine nature of love, especially erotic love, and also, as an objectified and

---

3. David Carr, "A Passion for God: A Center in Biblical Theology," *Horizons in Biblical Theology* 23 (2001): 1–24; Jonathan Kaplan, *My Perfect One: Typology and the Rabbinic Interpretation of the Song of Songs* (New York: Oxford University Press, 2015); Jon D. Levenson, *The Love of God: Divine Gift, Human Gratitude, and Mutual Faithfulness in Judaism* (Princeton: Princeton University Press, 2020), esp. 125–42.

4. Larry Lyke, *I Will Espouse You Forever: The Song of Songs and the Theology of Love in the Hebrew Bible* (Nashville: Abingdon, 2007).

mistreated creation of male writers and editors, embodies the domination of this feminine love.

Because of the troubling portrayal of love and women in the Song of Songs, this book serves as the best encapsulation, the culmination, of the understanding of love in the Hebrew Bible. Song 8:6–7, which many argue is the "climax of the poem and its raison d'être,"[5] best exemplifies the confusion and tensions that surround love:

> Set me as a seal upon your heart, as a seal upon your arm, for love is strong as death, passion fierce as the grave. Its flashes are flashes of fire, a raging flame. Many waters cannot quench love, neither can floods drown it. If one offered for love all the wealth of one's house, it would be utterly scorned.

The female protagonist, near the end of the poem, recites these beautiful lines about the power and mystery of love. In these verses, love is compared to fire ("flashes of fire"), indeed, a "raging" one, which is so awesome and enduring that it cannot be put out by "many waters," not even a "flood." These masterful verses, though they initially sound deeply romantic, actually reflect an uncertain and fraught vision of love. Love, according to these lines, is not wholly positive. Rather, if love is indeed an inextinguishable and everlasting flame, one which is incapable of being quenched with "many waters," not even by a "flood," then as much as love is Paradise, it is also Inferno. Like a raging forest fire, it is something that should be handled with extreme caution because it is dangerous, destructive, and uncontrollable, capable of wanton consumption, annihilation, and obliteration.

Indeed, the beauty and genius of this passage centers on its masterful ability to express love's awesome power—both the charm and allure of love as well as its terror and horror. As such, it is unsurprising that these verses keep comparing love and something like its opposite, that is, the thing that can extinguish love (8:7) to fraught things such as fire and water. Fire and water, on the one hand, are contrasts. Water can be used to put out fires, for example. On the other hand, fire and water are also similar in their capacity to both give life and to take it. Both are deeply ambivalent in that fire and water are something needed to survive as human beings and therefore, at times, something one desperately desires. However, they are also something with the fearsome capacity to destroy. When there is too much fire or too much water, all living things suffocate, burn, drown, and die. Water and fire, like the love to which

---

5. J. Cheryl Exum, *Song of Songs*, Old Testament Library (Louisville: Westminster John Knox, 2005), 245.

they are compared, are divinely potent and powerful, capable of creation and destruction.

So equally fraught and complicated, maybe even more so, are love and death, which are analogized: "for love is strong as death, passion fierce as the grave" (Song 8:6). This comparison between love and death, which is found in other literatures and cultures, again reflects both ecstasy and horror.[6] Death, for example, is strong because it is eternal and limitless. Its power comes from the fact that once something dies, it remains dead. It is pitiless and cannot be bargained with: as with love, you cannot buy your way out of it (8:7). Yet death and its power, though respected and feared, is precisely what the biblical text, through its narrative, continually tries to overcome and thwart, and, at points, even succeeds in doing. As Jon Levenson observes, the Hebrew Bible is filled with the hope of and instances of resurrection—an attempt to undo or break the chains of death and the very power it has.[7] Death is something in the Bible that should and can be overcome.

So what, then, are the writers saying when they compare love to death? What does it mean that love is like death in its power? Is love, like death, something so awesome and terrifying that it is something we hope to thwart? Or does the analogy work in the opposite direction in that love is something in opposition to or against death, something that can match death and therefore hopefully overcome it? What is the writer trying to say about the relationship between love and death with these verses?

This comparison between love and death purposely offers dissonant and contradictory messages and visions of love. In so doing, they serve as means through which to ask questions about love and the forces to which it is likened. Let us look again at the comparison between love and death in Song 8:6. One interpretation of this comparison is that love, like death, is just as eternal, strong, durable, and limitless. Therefore, love can match death and, as such, maybe even counter it in that even death cannot end love—an especially poignant understanding of love for those who have lost loved ones and yet who continue to love them. Yet going deeper, through this analogy, Song 8:6 also hints of a more complicated and disturbing relationship between love and death: death is precisely what gives love its enduring power, that love is not a rival or combatant of death, but its partner, its kin—its lover, as it were. Love and death are similar in power precisely because they are intertwined.

---

6. On the comparison between love and death found in other literatures and cultures, see Danilo Verde, *Conquered Conquerors: Love and War in the Song of Songs* (Atlanta: SBL Press, 2020), 3–4.

7. Jon D. Levenson, *Resurrection and the Restoration of Israel: The Ultimate Victory of the God of Life* (New Haven: Yale University Press, 2008).

As Michael Fishbane succinctly notes, "Love is also like death because it (too) sharpens awareness of the finitudes and fortunes of existence."[8]

Dan Werner draws out this connection between love and death in his examination of Plato's *Symposium*. Werner argues that, according to Plato, love and death are connected because: (1) love causes or compels peoples to die for those whom they love (i.e., sacrifice); (2) love stems from a desire for wholeness, that is, oneness, a desire to fuse with the lover and therefore, as such, that love actually entails a kind of death of the autonomy or the distinct self; and (3) "we love because we are mortal, and that we are seeking immortality (or at least something approaching immortality)."[9] Though Werner qualifies Plato's points, he, like Fishbane, at the end seems to connect love and death by arguing that it is precisely death or mortality that "lends urgency and intensity to our loves": "As with everything else in life that is scarce, we value and prize our loved ones in large part because we know that they cannot be with us forever. An immortal life would lack this dimension."[10]

The poem in Song 8:6–7 winks to this link between love and death, and relatedly, immortality and mortality, through its subtle references to the gods, especially the battles and contests between them. In particular, as interpreters have noted, Song 8:6–7, through its mention of death (*mavet*), water/flood, and "flashes" (*reshef*), alludes to the ancient Near Eastern combat myth whereby a storm god battles other gods such as Death (Mot) and various water deities, such as Lord River or Tiamat.[11] Though not envisioned as an outright enemy of the storm god, Reshef, translated as "flashes," also likely refers to "a god or agent of plague" (hints of this are also present at other points such as Deut. 32:24 and Hab. 3:5).[12]

If love is compared to Reshef (flashes of fire) and to Mot (death), these references to other deities and myths raise the question and the possibility as to whether love itself is also imagined as divine, as a god of sorts, and if so what kind of deity. That is, if love is a god or, I would argue, a goddess, in what realm does she belong—heaven or hell? Is she chthonic or ouranic and celestial? Is she aligned with death, drawing her powers from it, or set against

---

8. Michael Fishbane, *The JPS Commentary: Song of Songs* (Philadelphia: Jewish Publication Society, 2015), 209.

9. Dan Werner, "Love and Death," in *Immortality and the Philosophy of Death*, ed. Michael Chobi (Lanham: Rowman & Littlefield, 2016), 135–56 (143). Werner fills out the last point by arguing that, according to Plato, love stems not necessarily from our mortality but from our embodiment, though he admits that "human embodiment *entails* mortality" (145, emphasis original).

10. Werner, "Love and Death," 145.

11. Aren M. Wilson-Wright, "Love Conquers All: Song of Songs 8:6b–7a as a Reflex of the Northwest Semitic Combat Myth," *Journal of Biblical Literature* 134, no. 2 (2015): 333–45.

12. Fishbane, *Song of Songs*, 209.

death, actively attempting to thwart or overcome it? Or is love both? It is telling that the same confusion and ambivalence about love is also expressed about the woman (or women in general) in the Song of Songs. And as the woman is ambivalent—irreducible, ever-changing, mysterious, and unknowable—so also is love: mortal yet immortal, lethal yet life-giving, heavenly yet hellish, eternal yet temporary.[13]

THE QUESTION OF LOVE

The many stories about love we have examined, especially Song 8:6–7, through its use of images and metaphors, express the contradiction and complexities of love. Indeed, the Song of Songs is an appropriate and fitting encapsulation of the stories about love in the Hebrew text that we have explored. That is, like the tales of love, the statements about love in the Song of Songs are not really declarative statements but rather an expression of and a gateway to enduring questions: Is love really as strong as death? Is love death's companion or its enemy? Is love something to be desired, or is it to be avoided? Is it heaven or hell? Are mortals, those who are defined and limited, the only ones capable of love? Can the gods/God love and if so, how does their love differ, and what does it look like? Is love an intimate close union, or is it combat or a contest? Does love constitute an expansion of the self, or is it a loss of the self? Is love life-giving or lethal? Is love, especially erotic love, something that truly cannot be bought? Or is it something that has a price? Is love eternal or is it actually fleeting and temporary?

These stories about love raise these questions and, in so doing, evince a deep sense of uncertainty and struggle with love. Love is fraught and complicated, these stories tell us. And as such, love—like women to which its negative and most powerful effects are aligned—is neither one thing or another, but instead is irreducible, ever-changing, mysterious, and ultimately unknowable.

---

13. Though Eros is imagined as a child or as a young man, it is telling that Eros (in particular erotic love) is envisioned as having a dual nature: "Neither ignorant nor wise, neither beautiful nor ugly, neither mortal nor immortal, Eros is an intermediate figure" (Werner, "Love and Death," 142).

Bibliography

Ackerman, Diane. *A Natural History of Love*. New York: Random House, 1994.

Ackerman, H. C. "Saul: A Psychotherapeutic Analysis." *Anglican Theological Review* 3, no. 2 (1920): 114–24.

Ackerman, Susan. "The Personal Is Political: Covenantal and Affectionate Love (*'aheb, 'ahaba*) in the Hebrew Bible." *Vetus Testamentum* 52, fasc. 4 (2002): 437–56.

Ackerman, Susan. *When Heroes Love: The Ambiguity of Eros in the Stories of Gilgamesh and David*. New York: Columbia University Press, 2005.

Ackroyd, P. R. "The Verb Love—*'aheb* in the David Jonathan Narratives—A Footnote." *Vetus Testamentum* 25 (1975): 213–14.

Akiayama, Kengo. *The Love of Neighbour in Ancient Judaism: The Reception of Leviticus 19:18 in the Hebrew Bible, the Septuagint, the Book of Jubilees, the Dead Sea Scrolls, and the New Testament*. Leiden: Brill, 2018.

Alter, Robert. "Sacred History and the Beginnings of Prose Fiction." *Poetics Today* 1, no. 3 (1980): 143–62.

Amit, Yairah. *Hidden Polemics in the Biblical Narrative*. Translated by Jonathan Chipman. Biblical Interpretation Series 25. Leiden: Brill, 2000.

Amit, Yairah. "Literature in the Service of Politics: Studies in Judges 19–21." In *Politics and Theopolitics in the Bible and Postbiblical Literature*, edited by Henning Graf Reventlow, Yair Hoffman, and Benjamin Uffenheimer, 28–40. Journal for the Study of the Old Testament Supplement Series 171. Sheffield: Sheffield Academic, 1994.

Anderson, Gary A. *A Time to Mourn, A Time to Dance: The Expression of Grief and Joy in Israelite Religion*. University Park: Pennsylvania State University Press, 1991.

Arnold, Bill T. "The Love-Fear Antinomy in Deuteronomy 5–11." *Vetus Testamentum* 61, fasc. 4 (2011): 551–69.

Assis, Elie. *Identity in Conflict: The Struggle between Esau and Jacob, Edom and Israel*, Siphrut 19. Winona Lake: Eisenbrauns, 2016.

Auld, A. Graeme. *I & II Samuel: A Commentary*. Louisville: Westminster John Knox, 2011.

Avioz, Michael. "Could Saul Rule Forever?: A New Look at 1 Samuel 13:13–14." *Journal of Hebrew Scriptures* 5 (2005): n.p.

Bailey, Lloyd R. "The Cult of the Twins at Edessa." *Journal of the American Oriental Society* 88, no. 2 (1968): 342–44.

Barbiero, Gianni. *Song of Songs: A Close Reading*. Leiden/Boston: Brill, 2011.

Bechtel, Lyn M. "What If Dinah Is Not Raped? (Genesis 34)." *Journal for the Study of the Old Testament* 19, no. 62 (1994): 19–36.

Ben-Meir, Samuel. "Nabal, the Villain." *Jewish Bible Quarterly* 22 (1994): 249–51.

Ben-Noun, Liubov. "What Was the Mental Disease That Afflicted Saul?" *Clinical Case Studies* 2 no. 4 (2003): 270–82.

Berlin, Adele. "Characterization in Biblical Narrative: David's Wives." *Journal for the Study of the Old Testament* 23 (1982): 69–85.

Boswell, John. *Christianity, Social Tolerance, and Homosexuality: Gay People in Western Europe from the Beginning of the Christian Era to the Fourteenth Century*. Chicago: University of Chicago Press, 1980.

Boswell, John. *Same-Sex Unions in Premodern Europe*. New York: Vintage, 1994.

Boyle, Marjorie O'Rourke. "The Law of the Heart: The Death of a Fool (1 Samuel 25)." *Journal of Biblical Literature* 120, no. 3 (2001): 401–27.

Brenner, Athalya. *A Feminist Companion to the Song of Songs*. Sheffield: Sheffield Academic, 1993.

Brenner, Athalya. "Naomi and Ruth." *Vetus Testamentum* 33, no. 4 (1983): 385–97.

Brenner, Athalya. *The Israelite Woman: Social Role and Literary Type in Biblical Narrative*. Sheffield: JSOT Press, 1985.

Brenner, Athalya. "To See Is to Assume: Whose Love Is Celebrated in the Song of Songs?" *Biblical Interpretation* 1, no. 3 (1993): 265–84.

Brenner, Athalya, and Carole R. Fontaine, eds. *The Song of Songs: A Feminist Companion to the Bible*. Sheffield: Sheffield Academic, 2000.

Brettler, Marc Zvi. *The Book of Judges*. Old Testament Readings. London: Routledge, 2001.

Brueggemann, Walter. *Theology of the Old Testament: Testimony, Dispute, Advocacy*. Minneapolis: Fortress, 1997.

Cacioppo, Stephanie. *Wired for Love: A Neuroscientist's Journey Through Romance, Loss, and the Essence of Human Connection*. New York: Flatiron Books.

Cancian, Francesca M. "The Feminization of Love," *Signs: Journal of Women in Culture and Society* 11, no. 4 (1986): 692–709.

Carr, David. "A Passion for God: A Center in Biblical Theology." *Horizons in Biblical Theology* 23 (2001): 1–24.

Chapman, Cynthia R. *The Gendered Language of Warfare in the Israelite-Assyrian Encounter*. Harvard Semitic Monographs 62. Winona Lake: Eisenbrauns, 2004.

Clines, David J. A. "Why Is There a Song of Songs, and What Does It Do to You If You Read It?" In *Interested Parties: The Ideology of Writers and Readers*, 94–121. Sheffield: Sheffield Phoenix, 2009.

Coats, George W. *Genesis*. Vol. 1. Grand Rapids: Eerdmans, 1983.

Creangă, Ovidiu, ed. *Men and Masculinity in the Hebrew Bible*. Sheffield: Sheffield Phoenix Press, 2010.

Cross, Frank Moore. *From Epic to Canon: History and Literature in Ancient Israel*. Baltimore: Johns Hopkins University Press, 1998.

Dasen, Veronique. "Becoming Human: From the Embryo to the Newborn Child." In *The Oxford Handbook of Childhood and Education in the Classical World*, edited by Judith Evans Grubbs and Tim Parkin, 17–39. New York: Oxford University Press, 2013.

Dijk-Hemmnes, Fokkelien van. "The Imagination of Power and the Power of Imagination: An Intertextual Analysis of Two Biblical Love Songs: The Songs of Songs and Hosea 2." *Journal for the Study of the Old Testament* 44 (1989): 75–88.

Dresner, Samuel. "Rachel and Leah: Sibling Tragedy or the Triumph of Piety and Compassion?" *Biblical Review* 6, no. 2 (1990): 22–27, 20–42.

Eskenazi, Tamara. "Michal in Hebrew Sources." In *Telling Queen Michal's Story: An Experiment in Comparative Interpretation*, edited by David J. A. Clines and Tamara C. Eskenazi, 157–74. Sheffield: Sheffield Academic, 1991.

Esler, Philip Francis. "The Madness of Saul: A Cultural Reading of 1 Samuel 8–31." In *Biblical Studies/Cultural Studies*, edited by J. Cheryl Exum and Stephen D. Moore, 220–62. Sheffield: Sheffield Academic Press, 1998.

Exum, J. Cheryl. "Desire, Love, and Romance in the Hebrew Bible." *Oxford Research Encyclopedia of Religion*. https://doi.org/10.1093/acrefore/9780199340378.013.54.

Exum, J. Cheryl. *Song of Songs*. Old Testament Library. Louisville: Westminster John Knox, 2005.

Exum, J. Cheryl. "Ten Things Every Feminist Should Know about the Song of Songs." In *The Song of Songs: A Feminist Companion to the Bible*, edited by Athalya Brenner, 24–35. Sheffield: Sheffield Academic, 2000.

Exum, J. Cheryl. *Tragedy and Biblical Narrative*. Cambridge, UK: Cambridge University Press, 1992.

Feldman, Yael S. "'And Rebecca Loved Jacob,' But Freud Did Not." *Jewish Studies Quarterly 1*, no. 1 (1993/94): 72–88.

Fewell, David Nolan, and David M. Gunn. *Gender, Power, and Promise: The Subject of the Bible's First Story*. Nashville: Abingdon, 1993.

Fewell, Dana Nolan, and David M. Gunn. "Tipping the Balance: Sternberg's Reader and the Rape of Dinah." *Journal of Biblical Literature* 110, no. 2 (1991): 193–211.

Firth, David G. "The Accession Narrative (1 Samuel 27–2 Samuel 1)." *Tyndale Bulletin* 58, no. 1 (2007): 61–81.

Fishbane, Michael. *The JPS Commentary: Song of Songs*. Philadelphia: Jewish Publication Society, 2015.

Fleming, Erin E. "Political Favoritism in Saul's Court: חפץ, נעם, and the Relationship between David and Jonathan." *Journal of Biblical Literature* 135, no. 1 (2016): 19–34.

Fleming, Erin E. "'She Went to Inquire of the Lord': Independent Divination in Genesis 25:22." *Union Seminary Quarterly Society* 60, no. 3 (2007): 1–10.

Fokkelman, J. P. *Narrative Art in Genesis: Specimens of Stylistic and Structural Analysis*. Amsterdam: Assen, 1975.

Frymer-Kensky, Tikva. "Law and Philosophy: The Case of Sex in the Bible." *Semeia* 45 (1989): 89–102.

Frymer-Kensky, Tikva. *Reading the Women of the Bible: A New Interpretation of Their Stories*. New York: Schocken, 2002.

Gafney, Wilda. *Womanist Midrash: A Reintroduction to the Women of the Torah and the Throne*. Louisville: Westminster John Knox, 2017.

George, Mark K. "Yhwh's Own Heart." *Catholic Biblical Quarterly* 64, no. 3 (2002): 442–59.

Gilmour, Rachelle. *Representing the Past: A Literary Analysis of Narrative Historiography in the Book of Samuel*. Leiden: Brill, 2011.

Gilmour, Rachelle. "Saul's Rejection and the Obscene Underside of the Law." *The Bible and Critical Theory* 15, no. 1 (2019): 34–45.

Glueck, Nelson. *Hesed in the Bible*. Translated by A. Gottschalk. Cincinnati: The Hebrew Union College Press, 1967.

Gordon, Cyrus H. "The Story of Jacob and Laban in the Light of the Nuzi Tablets." *Bulletin of the American Schools of Oriental Research* 66 (1937): 25–27.

Granzberg, Gary. "Twin Infanticide: A Cross-Cultural Test of a Materialistic Explanation." *Ethos* 1, no. 4 (1973): 405–12.

Gunn, David M. *The Fate of King Saul: An Interpretation of a Biblical Story*. Sheffield: JSOT Press, 1980.

Halpern, Baruch. *David's Secret Demons: Messiah, Murderer, Traitor, King*. Grand Rapids: Eerdmans, 2001.

Hamilton, Victor P. *The Book of Genesis: Chapters 18–50*. Grand Rapids: Eerdmans, 1990.

Hankoff, Leon D. "Why the Healing Gods are Twins." *The Yale Journal of Biology and Medicine* 50 (1977): 307–19.

Hartley, John A. *Genesis*. Peabody: Hendrickson, 2000.

Heacock, Anthony. "Wrongly Framed? The 'David and Jonathan Narrative' and the Writing of Biblical Homosexuality." *The Bible and Critical Theory* 3, no. 2 (2007): 1–22.

Helsel, Carolyn, and Song-Mi Suzie Park. *The Flawed Family of God: Stories of the Imperfect Families of Genesis*. Louisville: Westminster John Knox, 2021.

Heltzer, M. "New Light from Emar on Genesis 31: The Theft of the Teraphim." In *"Und Mose schrieb dieses Lied auf": Studien zum Alten Testament und zum Alten Orient. Festschrift für Oswald Loretz zur Vollendung seines 70*, edited by M. Dietrich and I. Kottsieper, 357–62. Münster: Ugarit-Verlag, 1998.

Heschel, Abraham Joshua. *God in Search of Man: A Philosophy of Judaism*. New York: Farrar, Straus and Giroux, 1983.

Hirsh, Jody. "In Search of Role Models." In *Twice Blessed: On Being Lesbian, Gay, and Jewish*, edited by Christie Balka and Andy Rose, 83–91. Boston: Beacon, 1989.

hooks, bell. *All About Love: New Visions*. New York: William Morrow & Company, 2001.

Horner, Thomas M. *Jonathan Loved David: Homosexuality in Biblical Times*. Philadelphia: Westminster, 1978.

Humphreys, W. Lee. "From Tragic Hero to Villain: A Study of the Figure of Saul and the Development of 1 Samuel." *Journal for the Study of the Old Testament* 22 (1982): 95–117.

Humphreys, W. Lee. "The Rise and Fall of King Saul: A Study of an Ancient Narrative Stratum in 1 Samuel." *Journal for the Study of the Old Testament* 8 (1980): 74–90.

Humphreys, W. Lee. "The Tragedy of King Saul: A Study of the Structure of 1 Samuel 9–31." *Journal for the Study of the Old Testament* 6 (1978): 18–27.

Hunt, Morton. *The Natural History of Love*. New York: Anchor Books, Doubleday, 1959.

Imray, Kathryn. "Love Is (Strong as) Death: Reading the Song of Songs through Proverbs 1–9." *Catholic Biblical Quarterly* 75, no. 4 (2013): 649–96.

Jeansonne, Sharon. *The Women of Genesis: From Sarah to Potiphar's Wife*. Minneapolis: Augsburg Fortress Press, 1990.

Jennings, Theodore W., Jr. *Jacob's Wound: Homoerotic Narratives in the Literature of Ancient Israel*. New York: Continuum, 2005.

Johnson, Benjamin. "The Heart of the Chosen One in 1 Samuel." *Journal of Biblical Literature* 131, no. 3 (2012): 455–66.

Kaminsky, Joel. "Humor and the Theology of Hope: Isaac as a Humorous Figure." *Interpretation* 54 (2000): 363–75.

Kaplan, Jonathan. *My Perfect One: Typology and the Rabbinic Interpretation of the Song of Songs*. New York: Oxford University Press, 2015.

Kaplan, Jonathan, and Aren M. Wilson-Wright. "How the Song of Songs Became a Divine Love Song." *Biblical Interpretation* 26 (2018): 334–51.

Korte, Anne-Marie. "Significance Obscured: Rachel's Theft of the Teraphim: Divinity and Corporeality in Gen. 31." In *Begin with the Body: Corporeality, Religion and*

Gender, edited by Jonneke Bekkenkamp and Maaike de Haardt, 157–82. Leuven: Peeters, 1998.

Kreuter, Jens A. "Warum liebte Isaak Esau?" *Biblische Notizen* 48 (1989): 17–18.

Kugel, James. *The Bible as It Was*. Cambridge: Belknap Press of Harvard University Press, 1997.

Lapsley, Jacqueline. "Feeling Our Way: Love for God in Deuteronomy." *Catholic Biblical Quarterly* 65, no. 3 (2003): 350–69.

Levenson, Jon D. "1 Samuel 25 as Literature and as History." *Catholic Biblical Quarterly* 40, no. 1 (1978): 11–28.

Levenson, Jon D. *The Death and Resurrection of the Beloved Son: The Transformation of Child Sacrifice in Judaism and Christianity*. New Haven: Yale University Press, 1993.

Levenson, Jon D. *The Hebrew Bible, The Old Testament and Historical Criticism: Jews and Christians in Biblical Studies*. Louisville: Westminster John Knox, 2012.

Levenson, Jon D. *The Love of God: Divine Gift, Human Gratitude, and Mutual Faithfulness in Judaism*. Princeton: Princeton University Press, 2020.

Levenson, Jon D. *Resurrection and the Restoration of Israel: The Ultimate Victory of the God of Life*. New Haven: Yale University Press, 2008.

Levenson, Jon D. *Sinai and Zion: An Entry into the Jewish Bible*. San Francisco: Harper SanFrancisco, 1985.

Levison, John R. "Holy Spirit." In *New Interpreter's Dictionary of the Bible*. Vol. 2. Edited by Katharine Doob Sakenfeld, 859–79. Nashville: Abingdon, 2007.

Levi-Strauss, Claude. *Introduction to a Science of Mythology*. Vol. 1, *The Raw and the Cooked*. Translated by John and Doreen Weightman. New York: Harper & Row, 1969.

Lewis, Theodore J. "The Ancestral Estate *(nahalat 'elohim)* in 2 Samuel 14:16." *Journal of Biblical Literature* 110, no. 4 (1991): 597–612.

Longman, Tremper, III. *The Song of Songs*. Grand Rapids: Eerdmans, 2001.

Luc, Alexander To Ha. "The Meaning of *'hb* in the Hebrew Bible." PhD diss. University of Wisconsin–Madison, 1982.

Lyke, Larry. *I Will Espouse You Forever: The Song of Songs and the Theology of Love in the Hebrew Bible*. Nashville: Abingdon, 2007.

Malul, M. "*'āqēb* 'Heel' and *'āqab* 'To Supplant' and the Concept of Succession in the Jacob-Esau Narratives." *Vetus Testamentum* 46, fasc. 2 (1996): 190–212.

McCarter, P. Kyle. "The Apology of David." *Journal of Biblical Literature* 99, no. 4 (1980): 489–504.

McCarter, P. Kyle. "The Historical David." *Interpretation* 40, no. 2 (1986): 117–29.

McCarthy, Dennis J. "Notes on the Love of God in Deuteronomy and the Father-Son Relationship between Yahweh and Israel." *Catholic Biblical Quarterly* 27, no. 2 (1965): 144–47.

McKay, J. W. "Man's Love for God in Deuteronomy and the Father/Teacher-Son/Pupil Relationship." *Vetus Testamentum* 22, fasc. 4 (1972): 426–35.

McKenzie, Steven L. *King David: A Biography*. New York: Oxford University Press, 2000.

Mendenhall, George E. "Covenant Forms in Israelite Tradition." *Biblical Archaeologist* 17, no. 3 (1954): 50–76.

Mendenhall, George E., and Gary A. Herion. "Covenant." In *Anchor Bible Dictionary*. Vol. 1. Edited by David Noel Freedman, 1179–1202. New York: Doubleday, 1992.

Mobley, Gregory. "The Wild Man in the Bible and the Ancient Near East." *Journal of Biblical Literature* 116, no. 2 (1997): 217–33.

Mobley, Gregory. *Samson and the Liminal Hero in the Ancient Near East*. New York: T&T Clark, 2006.

Moberly, R. W. L. "Toward an Interpretation of the Shema." In *Theological Exegesis: Essays in Honor of Brevard S. Childs*, edited Christopher R. Seitz and Kathryn Greene-McCreight, 124–44. Grand Rapids: Eerdmans, 1999.

Moran, William. "The Ancient Near Eastern Background of the Love of God in Deuteronomy." *Catholic Biblical Quarterly* 25, no. 1 (1963): 77–87.

Morgan, Douglas N. "Love in the Hebrew Bible." *Judaism* 5 (1956): 31–45.

Morris, Leon. *Testaments of Love: A Study of Love in the Bible*. Grand Rapids: Eerdmans, 1981.

Murphy, Roland E. *The Song of Songs: A Commentary on the Book of Canticles or the Song of Songs*. Hermeneia. Minneapolis: Fortress, 1990.

Neusner, Jacob. "The Virtues of the Inner Life in Formative Judaism." *Tikkun* 1, no. 1 (1986): 72–83.

Niditch, Susan. *Judges: A Commentary*. Louisville: Westminster John Knox, 2008.

Niditch, Susan. *My Brother Esau Is a Hairy Man: Hair and Identity in Ancient Israel*. New York: Oxford University Press, 2008.

Niditch, Susan. *A Prelude to Biblical Folklore: Underdogs and Tricksters*. San Francisco: Harper & Row, 1987.

Niditch, Susan. *War in the Hebrew Bible: A Study in the Ethics of Violence*. New York: Oxford University Press, 1993.

Nissinen, Martti. *Homoeroticism in the Biblical World*. Minneapolis: Fortress, 1998.

Nissinen, Martti. "Die Liebe von David und Jonatan als Frage der modernen Exegese." *Biblica* 80, no. 2 (1999): 250–63.

Noegel, Scott B. "Scarlets and Harlots: Seeing Red in the Hebrew Bible." *Hebrew Union College Annual* 87 (2016): 1–47.

Olyan, Saul. "'Surpassing the Love of Women': Another Look at 2 Samuel 1:26 and the Relationship of David and Jonathan." In *Authorizing Marriage? Canon, Tradition, and Critique in the Blessing of Same-Sex Unions*, edited by Mark D. Jordan, 7–16. Princeton: Princeton University Press, 2006.

Park, Song-Mi Suzie. "The Frustration of Wisdom: Wisdom, Counsel, and Divine Will in 2 Samuel 17:1–23." *Journal of Biblical Literature* 128, no. 3 (2009): 453–67.

Park, Song-Mi Suzie. "Left-Handed Benjaminites and the Shadow of Saul." *Journal of Biblical Literature* 134, no. 4 (2015): 701–20.

Peleg, Yaron. "Love at First Sight? David, Jonathan, and the Biblical Politics of Gender." *Journal for the Study of the Old Testament* 30, no. 2 (2005): 171–89.

Plath, W. G., and W. H. Hollow. *The Torah: A Modern Commentary*. New York: Union for Reform Judaism, 1981.

Polaski, Donald C. "What Will Ye See in the Shulammite? Women, Power and Panopticism in the Song of Songs." *Biblical Interpretation* 5, no. 1 (1997): 64–81.

Pratchett, Terry. *I Shall Wear Midnight*. New York: HarperCollins, 2010.

Pressler, Carolyn. "Wives and Daughters, Bond and Free: Views of Women in the Slave Laws of Exodus 21.2–11." In *Gender and Law in the Hebrew Bible and the Ancient Near East*, edited by Victory H. Matthews, Bernard M. Levinson, and Tikva Frymer-Kensky, 147–72. Sheffield: Sheffield Academic, 1998.

Rad, Gerhard von. *Genesis*. Translated by John H. Marks. Philadelphia: Westminster, 1961.

Rashkow, Ilona. *Taboo or Not Taboo: Sexuality and Family in the Hebrew Bible*. Minneapolis: Fortress Press, 2000.

Richter, Sandra L. *Epic of Eden: A Christian Entry into the Old Testament*. Downers Grove: IVP Academic, 2008.

Römer, Thomas, and Loyse Bonjour. *L'homosexualité dans le Proche-Orient ancien et la Bible*. Genève: Labor et Fides, 2005.

Rooke, Deborah W., ed. *A Question of Sex? Gender and Difference in the Hebrew Bible and Beyond*. Sheffield: Sheffield Phoenix Press, 2007.

Rouillard, H., and J. Tropper. "*Trpym*, rituels de guérison et culte des ancêtres d'après 1 Samuel XIX 11–17 et les textes parallèles d'Assur et de Nuzi." *Vetus Testamentum* 37, fasc. 3 (1987): 351–57.

Sakenfeld, Katharine Doob. "Love." In *The Anchor Bible Dictionary*. Vol. 4. Edited by David Noel Freedman, 375–81. New York: Doubleday, 1992.

Sakenfeld, Katharine Doob. "Loyalty and Love: The Language of Human Interconnections in the Hebrew Bible." *Michigan Quarterly Review* 22, no. 3 (1983): 190–204.

Sakenfeld, Katharine Doob. *The Meaning of* Hesed *in the Hebrew Bible: A New Inquiry*. Missoula: Scholars Press, 1978.

Sarna, Nahum. *Genesis=Be-reshit: the Traditional Hebrew Text with the New JPS Translation*. Philadelphia: Jewish Publication Society, 1989.

Schroer, Silvia, and Thomas Staubli. "Saul, David and Jonathan—The Story of a Triangle? A Contribution to the Issue of Homosexuality in the First Testament." In *A Feminist Companion to Samuel and Kings*, edited by Athalya Brenner, 22–36. Sheffield: Sheffield Academic, 2000.

Schuele, Andreas. "Heart." In *The New Interpreter's Dictionary of the Bible*. Vol. 2. Edited by Katharine Doob Sakenfeld, 764–66. Nashville, TN: Abingdon, 2007.

Sparks, Kenton L. *Ancient Texts for the Study of the Hebrew Bible: A Guide to the Background Literature*. Grand Rapids: Baker Academic, 2017.

Speiser, E. A. *Genesis*. Garden City: Doubleday, 1964.

Staubli, Thomas, and Silvia Schroer. *Body Symbolism in the Bible*. Translated by Linda M. Maloney. Collegeville: Liturgical Press, 2001.

Sternberg, Meir. *The Poetics of Biblical Narrative: Ideological Literature and the Drama of Reading*. Bloomington: Indiana University Press, 1985.

Stewart, Elizabeth. *Exploring Twins: Towards a Social Analysis of Twinship*. New York: St. Martin's Press, 2000.

Sweeney, Marvin A. "Davidic Polemics in the Book of Judges." *Vetus Testamentum* 47, fasc. 4 (1997): 517–29.

Tambasco, Anthony. "Love." In *The Collegeville Pastoral Dictionary of Biblical Theology*, edited by Carroll Stuhlmueller, 567–68. Collegeville: Liturgical Press, 1996.

Thompson, J. A. "The Significance of the Verb *Love* in the David-Jonathan Narratives in 1 Samuel." *Vetus Testamentum* 24, fasc. 3 (1974): 334–38

Trible, Phyllis. *God and the Rhetoric of Sexuality*. Philadelphia: Fortress, 1978.

Turner, Victor. *The Ritual Process: Structure and Anti-Structure*. New York: Routledge, 1969.

van der Toorn, Karel. "The Nature of the Biblical Teraphim in the Light of Cuneiform Evidence." *Catholic Biblical Quarterly* 52 (1990): 203–4.

Verde, Danilo. *Conquered Conquerors: Love and War in the Song of Songs*. Atlanta: SBL Press, 2020.

Vikander, Diana. "The Authenticity of 2 Samuel 1.26 in the Lament over Saul and Jonathan." *Scandinavian Journal of the Old Testament* 2, no. 1 (1988): 66–75.

Wallis, Gerhard. "אהב." In *Theological Dictionary of the Old Testament*. Vol. 1. Edited by G. Johannes Botterweck and Helmer Ringgren, translated by G. Wallis, 99–118. Grand Rapids,: Eerdmans, 1977.

Waterman, Leroy. *Royal Correspondence of the Assyrian Empire*. Ann Arbor: University of Michigan Press, 1930–36.

Weems, Renita J. *Battered Love: Marriage, Sex, and Violence in the Hebrew Prophets*. Minneapolis: Fortress, 1995.

Weinfeld, Moshe. "The Covenant of Grant in the Old Testament and in the Ancient Near East." *Journal of the American Oriental Society* 90, no. 2 (1970): 184–203.

Weinfeld, Moshe. *Deuteronomy and the Deuteronomic School*. Oxford: Clarendon, 1972.

Werner, Dan. "Love and Death." In *Immortality and the Philosophy of Death*. Edited by Michael Chobi, 135–56. Lanham: Rowman & Littlefield, 2016.

Whitelam, Keith. "The Defence of David." *Journal for the Study of the Old Testament* 29 (1984): 61–87.

Williams, Gillian Patricia, and Magdel Le Roux. "King Saul's Mysterious Malady." *Hervormde teologiese studies* 68, no. 1 (2012): 1–6.

Wilson, Nancy. *Our Tribe: Queer Folks, God, Jesus, and the Bible*. San Francisco: Harper SanFrancisco, 1995.

Wilson-Wright, Aren M. "Love Conquers All: Song of Songs 8:6b–7a as a Reflex of the Northwest Semitic Combat Myth." *Journal of Biblical Literature* 134, no. 2 (2015): 333–45.

Wiseman, D. J. "The Vassal-Treaties of Esarhaddon." *Iraq* 20, no. 1 (1958): i–ii, 1–99.

Wolde, Ellen van. "A Leader Led by a Lady: David and Abigail in I Samuel 25." *Zeitschrift für die alttestamentliche Wissenschaft* 114, no. 3 (2002): 355–75.

Wolde, Ellen van. *Reframing Biblical Studies: When Language and Text Meet Culture, Cognition, and Context*. Winona Lake: Eisenbrauns, 2009.

Wrangham, Richard W. *Catching Fire: How Cooking Made Us Human*. New York: Basic Books, 2009.

Wyatt, Nick. "The Story of Dinah and Shechem." *Ugarit-Forschungen* 22 (1991): 435–36.

Yarbrough, Glenn. "The Significance of *hsd* in the Old Testament." PhD diss., Southern Baptist Theological Seminary, 1959.

Yee, Gale A. *Poor Banished Children of Eve: Women as Evil in the Hebrew Bible*. Minneapolis: Fortress Press, 2003.

Zakovitch, Yair. *Jacob: Unexpected Patriarch*. Translated by Valerie Zakovitch. New Haven: Yale University Press, 2012.

Zehnder, Markus. "Exegetische Beobachtungen zu den David-Jonathan-Geschichten." *Biblica* 79, no. 2 (1998): 153–79.

Index of Scripture

Index of Subjects

CPSIA information can be obtained
at www.ICGtesting.com
Printed in the USA
LVHW081141030523
745820LV00003B/4